Slice of Life

by

Jon Stamford

ISBN 978-1-4716-2331-8

Set in 11 pt Bookman Old Style

Jon Stamford

Jon Stamford was educated at Marlborough College and The University of Bath. After some two decades in academic neuroscience, he was diagnosed with Early Onset Parkinson's Disease in 2006. Jon is a full-time writer-scientist and has published three scientific books. He is married with three children.

Praise for Slice of Life

I found it very entertaining (I do like the idea of magnetic L plates falling off at 70 mph) and informative (ever since Terry Pratchett mentioned Journey to Samarra in his let's-all-snuff-it lecture I have been wondering what he meant).

Nancy B-S (columnist)

Well I thought A Slice of Life was seriously good, not that I would have expected anything less from you. Ok, it had nothing to do with PD but I couldn't help thinking of Hunter Davies' Father's Day column that he used to write in Punch - the antics of various members of his family catalogued each month in a witty and erudite way.

Claudia F (freelance writer and editor)

I read every blog entry yesterday afternoon and have been raving about them to anyone who would listen since. You accomplish much - science and stories are perfectly intertwined and manage to entertain and inform without being lachrymose. I can't wait for the next installment.

Emma D (editor, social media expert)

(It) has had (us) in stitches, especially the one about the sparkly body glitter!

Zoe M (neuroscientist)

My oldest son, my wife, and I sat around our kitchen table tonight while I read your latest blog entry, "Christmas Present". We laughed until we cried. I love the phrases such as, "epileptiform abandon", "shaking mouse droppings from my slippers". I was especially tickled by your reference to Scrabble (a game to which I am addicted), and the reference to Gordon Ramsay brought images to my mind that left me weeping with laughter. Thank you for sharing your gift of humor with us this Christmas. I look forward to meeting the ghost of Christmas future.

Bob K (Positively Parkinson's website)

Quite brilliant as you are at writing, you have reduced what was a bit of a creative struggle this afternoon to an early evening of tears....I have just read your two most recent blogs and have had to down tools for the day. On an afternoon when my artistic flow has completely failed me ....your words have been heartening, provocative and upsetting all at once. I feel quite guilty gatecrashing the Parkinson's website, but just wanted to say thank you for what you've written.

Nicola H (Interior designer)

Really like this! will add to my favourites

Katie P (Editor of "The Parkinson", PDS magazine)

This is superb ... I really enjoyed reading it and chuckling over it. You certainly have the ability to write an interesting piece.

Veronica E (office administrator)

Hi – loved it! Look forward to the book...

Lyn P (archaeologist)

Great reading! I shall continue to dip in and out

Sara L (teacher)

Very cool, gave me a good giggle as I was skiving off work. Definitely a recognisable style there my friend.

Steve S (writer and musician)

Love (it). Magnetic ones peel off at 70. Brilliant. Was at a Burns Supper tonight ... with one of my pals who thinks your writing is superb.

Bryn W (Wobblywilliams website)

Also by Jon Stamford

Monitoring Neuronal Activity (1992)

Neuroprotection (1996)

*Instant Notes in Human Physiology
(with Daniel McLaughlin and David White, 2006)*

Newly diagnosed?

It crosses my mind that many of you reading this book may be doing so because you too have been diagnosed with Parkinson's and that you are perhaps looking for guidance or some indication that people can cope, and do cope, with this illness.

I have lived with this now for nearly five years and my best piece of advice to the newly diagnosed would be, in Douglas Adams's words "don't panic".

It is possible to live with this condition, and to thrive even. Although Parkinson's will change the things you do, and the way you do them, it will only stop you if you allow it to.

People often react to a diagnosis of Parkinson's in one of two ways. There is the path of destruction, or more accurately self destruction. Don't ask the question "why me?" because it will lead you nowhere. Besides it had to be someone.

Then there is the path of affirmation. Parkinson's will be with you every day and every night. It's an unwelcome houseguest, a squatter even. But until that glorious day when we can evict it from our lives, we would do well to make the best of it.

That's not to say that it's easy. It isn't. It's not to say that the path is smooth. Again it isn't. You have Parkinson's, but the Parkinson's does not necessarily have you.

You can be defeated or defined by this condition. Parkinson's can, in so many unexpected ways, give as much as it takes. It's up to you to enjoy those gifts. And you will. Believe me, you will.

For Mother,
who understood

Acknowledgements

I would like to thank 'Claire', 'Catherine', 'Alice' and 'Alex', who have generously – if sometimes inadvertently – provided much of the source material for this book.

Without their humour and ability to see the funny side, there would be no book

Claire – for showing me there is more than one funny side to a joke

Catherine – nobody enjoys slapstick more than you. Remember the windscreen wipers and the scissors...

Alice – simply the funniest person I know when you want to be. LMAO.

Alex – Let's face it, growing up with two big sisters takes a good sense of humour

The life of every man is a diary in which he means to write one story, and writes another; and his humblest hour is when he compares the volume as it is with what he vowed to make it.

James M. Barrie (1860 - 1937)

Preface

Parkinson's, or *paralysis agitans* to give its medical name, is a progressive neurodegenerative condition characterised by tremors, rigidity, slowness of movement and loss of balance.

Ten thousand people are diagnosed with Parkinson's each year in the UK and Parkinson's affects more than 100,000 UK citizens.

Although Parkinson's is often considered a disease of old age, more than 1 in 20 are diagnosed before the age of 40.

Despite the nature of the condition, Parkinson's does not kill and symptoms can be ameliorated by drugs, at least in the earlier stages.

Parkinson's is a life sentence not a death sentence.

Further information on Parkinson's can be obtained from:

The Cure Parkinson's Trust
www.cureparkinsons.org.uk

Parkinson's UK
www.parkinsons.org.uk

Introduction

Stop me if you've heard this one before but, like most writers, I never intended to write a book. Okay I have written science books in the past but that's not quite the same thing. Writing for scientists is a world removed from this. So when Bryn Williams, Wobbly Williams himself, the doyen of the Parkinson's community, asked me if I wanted to write a weekly column for his website I had reservations. Why would anybody be interested in reading my miscellaneous jottings on life with Parkinson's? But Bryn is nothing if not persuasive. So in August 2009, I started writing a column/blog. We called it *Slice of Life*.

And I found the writing helped. It helped me come to terms with my illness. I gather from my mailbox that it helped readers do the same but above all, it made people laugh. And in a condition like Parkinson's, you need all the laughs you can get.

Over the years that I've been writing, I've often been asked whether I had any plans to publish the columns. My answer has always been a clear and resolute 'no'. But again, I find my determination places me in a minority of one. So here it is. A year of my life, its ups and downs, its fun and games. A slice of life. Enjoy.

Jon Stamford

February 2012

Well this is a new experience for me. Writing a diary, that is. I've kept diaries in the past but they have tended to make me cringe on rereading them. Long tracts of pubescent angst. Or, put another way, drivel. So I'm a bit anxious about consigning my thoughts to paper, to the ether or wherever they end up.

So let's be clear, this is not a diary. In any case my teenage daughters reinforce the point. They say it's a blog but then they call a newspaper column a paper blog. Whatever it is -- a column, a blog or a book -- doesn't seem to matter. What's in a name anyway? As far as I'm concerned, it's just a vehicle for me to tell you about Parkinson's, family life and so forth. Claire, my wife thinks it's a good idea as I'm prone to ranting - thanks dear - and she feels it might get things off my chest!

So first things first - who am I and why would you want to read anything I wrote? Well my background is neuroscience. For many years I taught in a medical school and, you'll appreciate the irony, did research on Parkinson's. So you can imagine my reaction when diagnosed. Oh how I laughed. Not.

I left academia in 2003 (although I still have an honorary position) and now ply my trade as a medical editor, writer and part time artist.

So what else can I tell you? I have three children - two girls and a boy aged seventeen, fifteen and twelve. Incidentally, as a father, is there anything scarier than teenage daughters? My eldest, Catherine, is a keen musician while Alice, my younger daughter is into all things equestrian. Alex, my son is a keen cricketer. An ordinary family with ordinary worries.

My own sporting exploits extend about as far as some technically limited tail end batting for my local cricket team's 4th XI. I have a weakness for cheese, chocolate and red wine to the horror of my neurologist who visibly winces when I step on the scales. So I don't run for buses let alone marathons. I swim like a fish (of the battered variety with chips). And as for cycling, the sight of me in Dayglo Lycra is enough to stop traffic! Definitely not for the squeamish!

So now the formalities are over, what can you expect from me? In no particular order - music, cricket, diagnoses, medicines, impulse shopping, cars, tools, pubs, food and drink, shakes, people who are rude in shops, toys, politics, friends, family, grandparents, death, books, family holidays, drink, creativity, Christmas, pets, baboons, supermarkets, daytime television, Facebook, astronomy, gardening, camping, football, recipes, the Swiss Army knife, Latin teachers, foreign languages, moths, ghosts and why you will never get in the bathroom if you have teenage daughters. Weighty matters all.

September

Cricket and Cooking

1st September 2009 ~ Cricket!

Summer 2009 - as the Ashes reach their conclusion, I feel the need to talk about cricket.

Cricket has been an enduring passion of mine for as long as I can remember. At school, our first XI used to be a groundschool for the counties and pretty much everyone at school played cricket at some level. Like so many boys if my generation, I would listen to the radio's crackly test match commentaries during lessons on a discreet earpiece. When lessons were over I would spend hours bowling against tree stumps or dustbins. Cricket was, for me, the soundtrack of summer.

So, with this passion for the game, you might imagine that I would be quite good?

Wrong, so wrong.

Unlike Charlie my kid brother, who once had a trial for Yorkshire and bowled unplayable outswingers at blistering pace, I had no such sporting prowess. My fastest delivery was just as likely to thud into the ground at my feet as it was to fly over the wicket keeper without bouncing. I can still hear my brother laughing. I honestly believe that sledging was invented in our back garden around 1972. Never has there been such an unequal division of sibling sporting talent as between my brother and I!

When I left school in 1976, I left cricket behind. And it left me. It was a mutual and amicable separation. Sure I still listened to Test Match Special in the car and would often stop to watch a village cricket game for a few overs if I happened to pass by. And like all armchair cricketers I was always happy to offer an opinion on the England team selectors or umpiring vagaries if anyone cared to listen. But that was it. The years went by - my bat, cracked and long since forgotten, gathered mould in the attic while my grubby old whites were thrown away or torn up for dusters.

Fast forward thirty years.

Summer holidays 2006 and my son Alex, nine, is playing on his Gameboy, clearly intent on spending the entire holiday exercising little more than his thumbs. This is irritating my wife who feels that young boys, like puppies, need regular exercise - lots of it. Just as she is getting into her stride, her soliloquy is interrupted by the postman with the usual mix of bills and flyers for things I never knew I wanted. Most go straight in the bin but one catches my eye. "Cricket camp for under 11s" at a nearby village cricket club. Alex has never played cricket before but who cares - it fulfils his need for exercise, I think to myself. And the memsahib will be happy.

I shakily phone the number. It is still a good six months before I am diagnosed with PD and I am pinning the obvious tremors and stiffness on a rather over-refreshed pub quiz the night before (we came third since you ask). A man answers. Yes, there is one place left and the 'camp' starts today. Fifteen minutes later, we arrive at a picturesque ground and a grumpy Alex emerges from the car still muttering about high scores on Asteroids or Haemorrhoids or whatever it is called. Just as I open my mouth to lecture him about his attitude, a voice calls his name. It is a classmate and both are happy to see each other. I hand over a cheque to an earnest man in a tracksuit and drive off.

Four o'clock and it's time to pick him up. I arrive on the dot to be met by Alex, hands on hips. He mumbles something that, to anyone other than his parents, sounds like a series of grunts. Fortunately I speak Nineyearoldboy fluently and can translate this as "The coach wants to talk to you".

Uh oh.

Has he been in a fight? Stolen another boy's lunch money? I prepare an apology for each eventuality as the coach strides toward me. Brief introductions, then he gets to the point. "We think Alex is pretty good at cricket" he says "and wonder if he would like to join the club?" I am speechless for a while. "What does he do?" I ask eventually. The coach looks at me, puzzled.

"But surely you know already" he says "He's a fast bowler".

9th September 2009 ~ Dads and lads

Speaking as someone blessed with all the athletic prowess of a Galapagos tortoise, it has been fascinating to watch my son Alex's progress as a cricketer. From that first occasion three years ago, Alex (now twelve) plays regularly for the club's junior teams. When he isn't playing, he is in the nets. Even in winter.

Cricket doesn't stop in winter. No sirree! As I now know, there are indoor nets throughout the off-season and skills workshops and so on. My wife Claire works in London so most of the taxi duties inevitably fall to me as a homeworker.

After a while you get to know the other mums and dads (actually it's usually dads) and the coaches. Usually I sit in the gym's café with a coffee and a paper, half-aware of the whack of bat on ball or the shrieks of "owzat" from the boys in general or "OOOWWWZZZAAATTT" from Alex. He's always been a vocal cricketer!

So, last November, at the end of nets, Chris the head coach stopped me. "The club's putting together a dads and lads team next summer – would you be interested?" he asked.

I was caught off guard. "Er yes" I said "except for two little snags. Firstly, I haven't played any cricket in thirty six years...."

Chris interrupted. "Don't worry. It'll all come back to you. It's like riding a bike"

"And secondly" I continued "I have Parkinson's".

There was a pause. Chris looked me in the eye. "We guessed" he said quietly.

So we talked for a while. He made no promises, raised no false hopes. He was direct and honest. But if I was interested, I could give it a go at the 'Dads nets' in April.

Somehow, in my excitement, I had forgotten to mention the third snag – that I was rubbish at cricket anyway! Even before the PD.........Oops!

April came much too quickly. At the nets were a dads' army of cricketers in every shape and size. Despite this spectacular physiological variety, they all had one thing in common – they were much better at cricket than me! While they played cover drives of balletic beauty, I swiped and slashed at every ball like a hippo on roller skates. Over several weeks, my technical deficiencies as a batsman were ruthlessly exposed. I faced inswingers, outswingers, cutters, bouncers, yorkers and googlies, mostly accompanied by the sound of my stumps being clattered.

'Dads nets' finished in May. I was bruised and battered but at least I still had the same number of teeth and testicles as in April. More than anything, I was happy I had 'given it a go'. At the end of the last session Chris gathered us together and thanked us all for our efforts. I zipped up my kit bag and headed to the showers. It had been fun.

Alex was waiting outside leaning against a soft drinks machine.

"Where's Heathfield?" he asked.

"In Sussex" I replied "Why?"

"Because we are playing them on Saturday" he said "and Dad, you're batting at number seven".

I had to sit down.

And so the season began. For the first time in 36 years, I stood at the crease asking for "middle and leg" before clipping a tidy single to fine leg. Off the mark. Off the bloody mark!

With my shakes, I cut a strange figure in the field, as I stand trembling, shuffling from one foot to the other. But that's the thing with PD. The tremors vanish when you move. A quivering jelly can sometimes execute a spectacular diving catch – as I did in one game to the amazement of my team mates. And myself.

PD affects cricket in some strange ways. Some things are easy, others impossible. I cannot easily grip or release a cricket ball. So bowling is out of the question and my throwing is feeble. I tire easily so I need to field in close rather than chase the ball to the boundary.

The skipper understands - so I field at slip, gully or point. Sometimes the ball flies fast to me. But that's fine - reactions are often the last thing to go in PD, so my close catching is OK.

Batting is better against fast bowlers where it is mainly a case of quick reactions. I hate spinners – too long to think and make the wrong decision!

The team plays in the East Sussex Village League Division Twelve (there are only twelve divisions before you ask). There are ten teams in our division and, we finished tenth, having won a scant three of eighteen games. My own haul for the season has been a mere fifty two runs at an average of slightly over four. And one catch. Not exactly Kevin Pietersen! When you count the cost of equipment and match fees, I calculate that each of my runs has cost about a fiver! But I have loved every minute of it.

Best moment of the season? Shuffling past Alex's bedroom as my wife was saying goodnight to him after the Heathfield game "I'm so proud of Dad" he whispered.

Put a price on that!

21st September 2009 ~ Shake and bake!

It's been a puzzling few weeks in the Stamford household.

I'm not sure why but Catherine, our elder daughter, seventeen, has suddenly taken to cookery and baking. Mostly puddings and cakes. And mostly a diversion from homework or music practice methinks. Well put yourself in her place – 1000 word psychology essay on pecking behaviour in pigeons or a *tarte aux fraises* the size of a manhole cover?

Quite.

Still, this leaves me in a bit of a quandary over the balance between school and kitchen. On the one hand, homework is definitely taking second place to the cookery. On the other, we are now eating like pre-revolutionary French royalty. Life is suddenly a parade of pavlovas, a melee of meringue, a cornucopia of cakes.

And the essay? My normal response to inadequate homework is the Heavyhanded Disciplinarian Father Speech, delivered with what I fancy is Churchillian bearing "Never in the field of human homework has so little been done for so long".

You get the picture.

But this kind of oratory carries no weight when delivered by a man wiping lemon curd from his shirt. Nor will a teenage daughter take a lecture from a father holding an embarrassing large slice of Victoria sponge and spluttering cake crumbs while talking.

Insidiously, Parkinson's has robbed me of my natural gravitas (younger daughter Alice is sniggering as she reads this – wot gravitas?). Instead of sitting at the head of the table at dinner, punctuating the daily chatter and school gossip with *bon mots*, my attention is focussed nowadays on simply relaying food from plate to mouth.

"You're quiet" my friends will say as I battle with my meal like a pianist learning Rachmaninov. Nobody (outside the family) has yet offered to cut up my food but that day will doubtless come. In the meantime, I chart a messy course from meal to meal.

Parkinsonian tremors can turn the average meal into a challenge worthy of The Krypton Factor. On a bad day, peas are scattered to the four corners of the earth, soup usually gets no further than my lap while red wine targets my best white shirt like a cruise missile. Certainly, nothing much seems to find my mouth!

Our dog is no fool and has always taken up station near the messiest eater in the family. For many years that was Alex, who addressed his food with all the refinement of a velociraptor. At breakfast, lunch and supper, Flora would lie Sphinx-like waiting for the occasional morsel.

No longer. For many months now, Flora has not moved from my side at mealtimes. Nor does she lie down. No, she sits dribbling (much like me) by my side in the sure and certain hope of the manna to follow. She has the decency to look up at me with liquid brown eyes as though apologising. "Nothing personal" she seems to be saying "it's just business – and I'm hungry"

Mealtimes take on a comically unpredictable air. Always able to lighten even my darkest moods, my family guess openly how much food will end up on the floor. Rotigotine roulette if you will. Sometimes, like tipsters studying form, the kids will ask me when my last dose was taken or press Claire for details of the anticipated supper. For instance, a well-dosed Jon despatching a plate of sandwiches barely draws their attention. On the other hand, a tired and tremulous father facing Spaghetti Bolognese has them scurrying for the camcorder, with barely concealed glee. We take our seats, I reach for the parmesan and, ten seconds later, the table looks like a nativity scene. We are all sobbing with laughter.

Something must be done and the kids conclude that a bib is the way forward.

Alice and I go shopping. In Mothercare.

Alice: "You are going to behave Dad, aren't you"
Jon (*winks*): "Trust me" (*fiendish smile*)

Shop assistant enters, stage left

Mothercare shop assistant: "Can I help you?"
Jon: "Yes please - I need a bib."
MSA; "Certainly sir. Here is our range of bibs"

Daughter sniggers

Jon: "They all look very small to me"
MSA (*surprised*): "They are a standard size. How big do you need?"

Alice bites her tongue to stop herself laughing.

Jon (*glances round*): "What have you got in a 16" collar?"

October

Jags, Shaving & Holidays

1st October 2009 ~ Boys' toys

Almost my earliest childhood memory, nearly 50 years ago, is of standing at the windowsill with my mother, waving my father off to work each morning. We lived in Denham at the time and people did that sort of thing. But as my mother returned to the chores of the day, I would linger at the window watching the cars go by. Like most four year old boys, I could identify all makes of car. Had it been twenty years earlier, I would have been confidently telling Spitfires from Hurricanes, Messerschmitts from Heinkels and so forth. But this was 1961 and I had to settle for cars. Not just any cars mind you. Among the Austins and Morrises, Humbers and Singers, Rileys and Wolseleys, there were two I was looking out for. One was a green Volkswagen Karmann Ghia, which, with Teutonic precision, passed the house every day at exactly 8.32 AM. Even in the 1960s, the automotive industry's heyday, the Karmann Ghia looked special. But beautiful though it was with its coupe body and whitewall tyres, the Karmann Ghia was just a warm-up for the main event.

At around quarter to nine, to a fanfare in my head, Mr Potts, the local bank manager would leave for work. And he had a Jag.

A shiny green Jag with wire wheels that lived, like a caged beast, in his garage, never on the drive. Too often for my liking, a bank colleague would collect him, the Jag would stay in the garage, and I would slink, disappointed, back to my Frosties. But if I was lucky and especially if it was summer, Mr. Potts would fire up the Jag. And although we were ten houses away, we would hear its distinctive sound, somewhere between a snarl and a purr. To anyone else it just sounded like a powerful car. But to a motor-obsessed four year old, this was not just a powerful car: this was a six cylinder, 3.4 litre Mark II Jaguar capable of nought to sixty in 11.5 seconds and with a top speed over a hundred miles per hour. Grace, space and pace.

Indeed this was the car for anyone interested in banking - not only did Mr Potts the bank manager drive a Jag, but so too did the likes of Buster Edwards, a man with an equally consuming interest in the workings of the average high street bank. The Mark II Jag was, after all, the favoured getaway car of most sixties villains.

I may only have been four years old but I wanted a Jag. If I had to wait, fine. I could be patient if necessary. Even buy other cars too as I grew up. Sensible practical cars. Hatchbacks with cup holders and parking sensors. Family cars with folding seats and leaking sunroofs. All of these.

But somewhere, garaged at the back of my mind all along was Mr Potts's Jag.

Now one of the more dispiriting diversions of PD is the need to declare the condition to the DVLA whose robotic, if understandable, response is to cancel your existing licence and replace it, at their discretion, with a short term licence, renewable on medical advice.

This focusses the mind. Not 'arf!

When you realise your motoring days could end at any moment with a stroke of the DVLA's pen, each motoring mile becomes more precious. Open roads become more liberating, traffic jams more frustrating. Somehow all motoring senses are heightened. So when the DVLA gave me my three- year licence, I metaphorically consigned the boring cars to the bin. If I had only three years of motoring left, I was damn well going to enjoy them.

It was Jag Time and I told the wife so.

'Unimpressed' barely covers Claire's response.

A few trenchant sentences left me in no doubt about my fiscal responsibilities as father and husband and where the Jag fitted into them. It didn't.

No, the order of priorities was new kitchen, new bathroom, garden landscaping and so on. Buying a Jag was about seventieth on the starting grid of tasks, somewhere between unblocking the patio drain and neutering the guinea pig.

By the time I had reassessed the grid, and carefully weighed all the arguments, the Jag was back on pole.

Now the difficult part. How do you buy a Jag with only ten grand to spend? Assuming you exclude Buster's fast track approach to Jag ownership.

As it happens, one of the less widely publicised features of Jaguars is their jawdropping depreciation, a hangover from the sixties rustbucket days. While most German metal holds its worth like Chris Bonnington clinging to a rock face, merely turning the ignition key in a Jaguar seems inexplicably to halve its resale value. Very bad if you buy new. But very good if, like me, you can only afford to buy a used Jag.

Even so, ten grand Jags are about as common as solar eclipses.

I phoned the local Jag dealer and explained to the salesman that I needed an S-type, that curvy retro homage to the Mark II, for under ten grand. I could swear he put me on speakerphone.

I didn't think they were ever going to stop laughing.

Slowly it dawned on the salesman that this wasn't a prank call. I really did want an S-type for peanuts. He apologised and said he would look. It might take a while.

"Don't worry" I said "I've waited decades, what's another few weeks"

To be honest I didn't expect to hear from him again but, as good as his word, he searched. Two weeks later, he found a 3 litre zircon blue S-type and brought it to my house to test drive. I heard it pull up.

Suddenly it was 1961 and I was a four year old boy again.

I sat in the driver's seat and took in the acres of leather and forests of maple that had made this car. I turned the ignition and revved it. Ten minutes later we were sorting out the paperwork. A week later I was collecting it.

"Any advice on driving?" I asked the dealer.

"It's a Jag" he said "Drive it like you stole it"

8th October 2009 ~ Dicing with death...

To a middle aged man with two teenage daughters, the bathroom is not so much a temple of cleanliness as a gender battleground. Outnumbered and outgunned, my chances of uninterrupted toiletry are negligible – even assuming I can get in the bathroom in the first place. Angry hammering on a locked bathroom door is about as futile as a daylight assault on Spion Kop

So, in true military fashion I attempt to steal a march on the enemy. I wake early and capture the bathroom before the Boers – sorry, my daughters – establish a bridgehead.

Even so, the bathroom is a minefield, a hostile place full of unseen dangers. Everywhere there are bewildering balms, salves, and unguents - more lotions and potions than a Harry Potter book. Nothing is what it seems nor where it should be. My own soap, antiperspirant, shaving cream and toothpaste are on the floor or in the bin. It is as though Jonny Wilkinson has used my toiletries to practice drop kicks.

In the half light of an autumn dawn, morning ablutions are akin to playing Russian roulette. You pay a high price for any momentary lapses of concentration. Too often I fumble blindly for the shower gel and lather myself liberally in whatever it is. Ten minutes later as I bellow out the end of Nessun Dorma, I am tinglingly clean, but smell like a tropical fruit plantation. And my body is covered in glitter.

More than once, I have brushed my teeth with sunscreen or even, as on one exquisitely unsettling morning, with a new tube of haemorrhoid ointment.

Believe me, you never quite forget the taste of Preparation H.

When I mention this confusion to my neurologist, his pen visibly hovers over the dementia box on his checklist until I explain. "Teenage daughters" I say. "Aaah" he nods wearily "Say no more".

Teenage girls, I have discovered, don't use soap either, preferring instead faddy facial cleansers made with bits of the rainforest that even the animals ignore. I have long since given up looking for my bar of carbolic and now simply help myself to the gritty apricot scrub. Most mornings I already smell like Carmen Miranda's hat and glitter like a 1970s disco mirrorball. It couldn't get much worse.

Actually it could get a whole lot worse. And for one friend with similarly aged daughters, it did.

Lurking unseen among the exfoliants in his bathroom was a tube of depilatory cream. You know the stuff – designed to eliminate hairy legs. It also makes short work of eyebrows. One minute he's Denis Healey, the next he's Niki Lauda.

Like I said, it's a battleground. Even my son Alex, previously my staunchest ally in The War of The Bathroom, shows signs of deserting me. Claire and I think he has "a girlfriend". What else could account for the transformation of a previously hydrophobic twelve year old into the shower monster, a boy barely visible though a haze of body spray. And he is using my aftershave. I don't begrudge him the odd splash but he seems to be using it as a marinade.

But all of these toiletry tribulations pale compared to my biggest bathroom trauma.

Shaving.

I've always been a wet shaver. I like the calm zen-like ritual as much as anything else. And, although I am oblivious to most grooming products, this one area has consistently engaged my attention. For the last thirty years, I have used the same sandal and cedarwood shaving cream applied with a handmade badger brush and I shave with an old fashioned single bladed razor I bought in 1982 from a shop in Knightsbridge. Not that I'm obsessive, you understand.

Irrespective of one's preferred blade, the problem is this. Shaking and shaving do not sit well together. An unexpected tremor as the blade glides below the chin and suddenly I look like an extra in a Martin Scorcese film. I don't mind the odd nick – that's par for the course – but cuts the size of Prussian duelling scars really don't set you up for the day.

So I am stuck between Scylla and Charybdis. Do I grow a beard or find a way of shaving that does not mean driving to work via the blood bank?

The beard does not seem an option. Where I see distinguished, grizzled charm others only see Worzel Gummidge. Besides, says Claire, I frighten children. Nor does designer stubble work for me. I think you have to be Italian. Certainly Claire was unconvinced "What designer have you used?" she asked "Jackson Pollock?"

So an electric shaver it has to be. Like surrendering a driving licence, this is a watershed moment, a recognition that my throat cannot take any more Sweeney Todd mornings. Even so, I take the step grudgingly. Currys has shelves of razors with names like Predator, Wolverine or Pagan. I yawn. I can't pretend I am even interested in the comparative merits of the Phillips Valhalla 5 or the new Braun Gonad. Ok, I made up the names but you get the drift. I eventually plump for a Swivel Headed Turbo Hyper Mach 25 Vibro Megablade or something like that. Who cares. Although it has more power than a family hatchback, it plucks rather than cuts and is noisier than a space shuttle launch.

The best a man can get? I think not.

16th October 2009 ~ Books

Bookshops are among my favourite places on the planet. I am unable to walk past - I have to go inside. Once inside, I am unable to leave without buying. Everything from biographies of 1930s opera stars to War Poets, from genealogy to canal boat crafts, from Ernest Hemingway to Bill Bryson. Secondhand bookshops are the best. I love their dusty ramshackle labyrinths. In Hay on Wye this year, I thought I had died and gone to Heaven.

Books are everywhere at home. The shelves creak with fact and fiction, tome and pamphlet. Piles of books stand like Neolithic cairns in corners and under tables. Books tumble from cupboards and wonkily support beds. Boxes of books fill the loft and garage. I counted more than five hundred books in the bedroom alone.

So this shocked me when I read it the other day. Apparently something like a quarter of all the households in Britain have five or fewer books. Five or fewer! I had to read it twice too.

It gets worse.

The same survey found that people spend, on average, about four hours a week reading. About thirty five minutes a day. At first that doesn't seem *too* worrying. Until you realise that's *all* reading - everything from the microwave instructions on a Chicken Chow Mein to the closing stanzas of The Waste Land. The article didn't distinguish. As far as the survey was concerned, they are cut from the same cloth. Reading is reading. A flyer advertising pizza delivery is the same as Finnegan's Wake

So all those years spent by writers penning the greatest works of literature were pointless. They might as well have been writing biscuit wrappers. I can just imagine TS Eliot chewing his pencil as he mulled over where to insert that critical Wagner quotation into the washing instructions for a mohair jumper. Why did Tolstoy fritter away his life on War and Peace when he could have been crafting the fine print on Costa Brava timeshare contracts. And wouldn't Kerouac's stream of consciousness prose have been better suited to listing the ingredients of Red Bull than the nomadic habits of the Beat generation. Wasted lives all.

The same survey went on to say that airport bookshops account for more than half of all books sold annually in the UK. The prospect of sun, sand and sangria is unthinkable without a bodice-ripper to cuddle up to. If you are a woman that is. Men's preferred reading matter involves deadly virus strains spread by killer zombies. That sort of thing.

And men, it transpires, mostly read on the toilet. Ponder that for a minute. The greatest works of literature being read to a continuo of grunts and groans. Not so much writing for posterity as for the posterior. Imagine reading

Sharma's account of Queen Victoria's reign whilst on the throne oneself.

I could go on.

Time for my medicine (says the wife).

Since developing Parkinson's, I have stopped taking books and reading for granted. No longer do I squirrel books away for a rainy day. These are the rainy days. Books have become even more precious and my time with them is cherished.

Strangely, the mere act of reading has evolved from a purely mental exercise into something altogether more unusual. Let me explain. Firstly, my eyes will not focus on close objects. By gradual degrees, I have turned into my father, whose attempts to read the Telegraph with arms extended like a robot would so amuse his children. Inspector Gadget extendable arms would help but are almost certainly unavailable on the NHS.

Glasses then. A pair of reading glasses or bifocals and all is sorted – right? Well, no actually. Being able to focus on letters is certainly helpful. But this is not an eye examination. Imagine if your optician, instead of holding the card still, shook it violently and unpredictably from side to side. Not so easy now huh? And therein lies the problem. If I can rest the book on my lap, the text is still and the pages pass by, like scenery viewed from a train. But if I have to hold a book unsupported, such as on a packed tube, the tremors take over and reading is like trying to land a biplane on the Ark Royal in a hurricane. Descriptive passages are reduced to snapshots and critical narrative details are lost in the neurological chaos. More than once I have reached the last page of a novel only to find the denouement in the hands of a character entirely new to me.

The solution, I find, is to make small hand movements as I feel each tremor starting. Voluntary trumps involuntary every time. It resets the clock for a few seconds and allows me to read something more narratively sophisticated than a shampoo label. Put all this together and reading while standing on a train is now a full body workout as I bend knees to prevent cramps, extend arms to their limit and clench and unclench my hands. Read–two-three-and-breathe-two-three. I can almost see Olivia Newton John singing "Physical". And relax.

But it's not all bad – the survey found that women were attracted to men who were well read. Did I mention my thousands of books?

Okay ladies - form an orderly queue!

22nd October 2009 ~ Holidays (part 1)

Nearly all of us Parkies experience sleep problems at various times. My times are about five in the morning. I wake to the sound of foxes playing in the streetlights outside and immediately my mind is whirring. I cannot keep my eyes open but I cannot sleep either. It's a problem frankly. These are the dark hours before dawn, filled with brooding imaginings and flitting shadows.

And nothing is more unwelcome a novelty than this to someone who has previously slept like Rip van Winkle. I slept through the 1987 hurricane. I was unaware of the Baltic Exchange bombing. I would probably have snored through the blitz. Most discouraging of all, this insomnia does not respond to my favourite trio of tranquillisers – Lagavulin, Ardbeg and Talisker. Whilst a near-perfect coda to the working day, they are a much less sensible overture.

It wasn't always thus. As a young lad, I was Prince Morpheus, the doyen of dozing. There were only two days each year when I woke before the rest of the family. One was Christmas. The other was the first day of the family holiday.

My parents had not yet been bitten by the foreign travel bug, so holidays in the 1960s meant Devon or Cornwall. Even so, compared with Doncaster's coal grime, the palm trees of Penzance were unimaginably exotic. With my toes in warm golden sand, watching boats on a sapphire sea it was hard to believe this was even the same country. It was a far cry from the salty sting of Skegness in spring or the wind-lashed grey green breakers of Bridlington.

But I'm jumping ahead. The countdown to the holiday followed a rigid pattern. First, our holiday clothes were washed and packed. For a week before the holiday, we were urchins, wearing our oldest clothes - tatty ill-fitting garments from the bottom of the drawer, clothes in that limbo between wardrobe and duster. Mother had packed everything else into the same demob suitcases that we had always used. In fact, the same ones my grandparents had used. We knew how to travel in style.

By eight, my father was pushing large suitcases into a small car boot. An hour later, red-faced and dripping, he was still trying to do so, by now punctuating the pushes with the occasional kick. Fortunately I couldn't lipread. "Should I offer to help?" I asked my mother. "Best not" she said.

When my father had finally bludgeoned the surviving suitcases into the boot, we would leave. After some five minutes we stopped, my father would sigh and we turned round. Ten minutes later, after satisfying himself that he had, after all, locked the front door, we would again be on our way.

Twenty miles into a three hundred mile odyssey, my sister Venetia would blearily ask "How much further?", innocently triggering the usual series of ill-prepared pastimes. My father soon stopped encouraging us to "sleep and the journey would pass quickly". We couldn't and it didn't. We were too excited. I could almost feel the sand between my toes. We wanted the journey over.

By ten o'clock, Charlie, Venetia and I were bickering. By ten thirty we were brawling, openly trading punches across the back seat of the car while my father would briefly quell the riot by threatening to turn round again.

My mother would respond cheerily with I Spy. Although young children have an insatiable appetite for the game, the same cannot be said of adults. My mother, with the patience of Saint Theresa, would still feign astonishment as, year after year, C turned out to be car and R was road. Even my father would amuse himself, flippantly offering words like Sarcophagus, Homunculus and Velocipede. Thank goodness, he never played Scrabble

Still, there is a limit to how much "I Spy" any adult can reasonably be expected to play before losing the will to live. Eventually as scuffles broke out over spelling, my father would suggest we keep our eyes peeled in silence and shout out when we first saw the sea. And only then.

We were on the M1. Near Coventry. And my father knew it.

An hour passed before we lost interest in being Trappists and resumed the business of needling each other.

Then there were the boiled eggs. The night before our holiday, mother boiled several thousand eggs for the journey. Actually it was only ten, two each, but it seemed many more. My father had read an account of Sherman's march though Georgia and fretted over the availability of food on the holiday roads. So rather than have his children foraging and pillaging their way to Cornwall, we would travel three hundred flatulent miles south, in sulphurous abandon. Cars had no air conditioning in the 1960s and my father disliked the noise from open windows. To amuse us he would crack each egg on his elbow, the steering wheel, or even his forehead, sending us kids into fits of giggles.

And ice cream. My father, a GP, had a bee in his bonnet about the soft whippy stuff from vans. Very occasionally we would stop for one, against his better judgement. While I would be excitedly taking orders from the family to a distorted jangle of Greensleeves, my father would mutter under his breath about the likely pathogen content, words meaningless to a six year old. Finally I would reach the front of the queue.

"Three oysters, a 99 and a salmonella please"

"You trying to be funny lad?"

"No sir". I turned to my father "You did say salmonella didn't you dad?" My father looked at me. Then at the burly ice cream seller now rolling up his sleeves. "Run" he whispered. I looked back blankly. "Run now".

Back on the road emptyhanded.

Then Charlie would need the toilet. He would announce this, with the split-second timing of all great comedians, immediately *after* we had passed the slip road to the motorway services. Typically, Charlie passed from blithe comfort to legs-crossed, genitalia-clutching agony in about five minutes. When Charlie said he needed the toilet, you were ill-advised to enter into a protracted discussion. This was no time for a detailed risk assessment. Charlie was a ticking bomb. More than once he disembarked from a still moving car as we screeched to a halt outside a Little Chef.

Latterly, we travelled with a bucket. A prescription for disaster, if ever there was one. After three hours of fizzy drinks, the bucket was fuller than the petrol tank, my siblings and I were hyperkinetic, and my father was driving with uncharacteristic caution. It was inevitable that a lorry would pull out suddenly, my father would swerve to avoid it and the rear foot wells would be engulfed in a tsunami. Charlie and I singing Yellow Submarine probably didn't help. The bucket experiment was never repeated.

Eventually the nervous excitement would take its toll and we children would slip into slumber, leaving my parents free to eat up the miles with discussions of more mundane timbre as we children dozed. Warwickshire became Gloucestershire, then Somerset, Devon and eventually Cornwall.

Finally, after six hours of somnolence, Venetia would suddenly sit bolt upright and let out a piercing shriek. With wheels locked, the car came to rest, askew in a cloud of dust and rubber. My father, slumped over the steering wheel, tried to catch his breath. "What is it?" he asked.

"Look dad" she pointed "the sea!"

27th October 2009 ~ Dates

No I don't mean the shrivelled toffeed fruits in oval boxes with pictures of silhouetted camels and palm trees. Nor do I mean those popcorn-perfumed matinees in the back row of the Odeon stalls, trying to steal a kiss from your sister's best friend as the ushers played their torches along the rows.

I mean significant points in time and memory. Birthdays, anniversaries, that sort of thing. The events that provide the fixed points of reference around which we flesh out our lives.

"Well, it must have been 1978, if you ask Sharon, because her aunt Doris was in hospital after her hysterectomy, and Wayne was still waiting for a new probation officer."

"Lavinia says it was definitely 1981 because Tarquin had just been made president of the golf club and Camilla still had that blue Bentley."

Perhaps not exactly this, but you see my point.

Like most men, I remember a handful of dates such as family birthdays and our wedding anniversary. Without fail. Well, most times. Ok, more often than not.

Claire, on the other hand, remembers everything. Her memory is like a medieval lexicon of event-related information. Everything else is stored in a filofax the thickness of a breeze block. In family terms, this is the Ark of the Covenant, the repository of all birthdays, anniversaries, feast days, parents evenings, school holidays and significant dates in history. Claire knows when everyone was hatched, matched or despatched.

On a typical evening, as I wrestle with the plot of CSI, she briefs me when to send birthday cards and to whom.

"Next Thursday is Charlie's fortieth birthday. I have arranged a present. You just need to buy a card".

She stops. After a few seconds I am vaguely aware that a response is needed.

"Charlie?"

"Your brother".

"I have a brother?"

This sort of flippancy does not go down well.

But the point is this - I don't remember dates. My sort of memory is different, more pictorial, more sensory.

Give you an example.

I remember when my eldest, Catherine, was born on a frozen January night nearly eighteen years ago. As Claire huffed and puffed in the delivery room, the midwife sent me to fetch a bag from the car. It was three o'clock in the morning. I remember my billowing breath forming Halloween orange clouds in the mercury glare of the street lamps. I remember the stillness broken only by the crackle of my frosty footsteps echoing from dark slumbering buildings, strands of leftover tinsel taped to windows. The moon, impossibly bright, like a hole punched in an ink-black sky. Running my finger through the frost on my car. The stale smell of yesterday's cooking as I passed the canteen. All this I remember.

And I remember Catherine in her mother's arms, greeting that first frosty morning with her dark eyes open, alert and penetrating, drinking in her surroundings. Fixing me in her gaze, she gave a flicker of acknowledgement as though saying "We have known each other forever"

I also remember visiting the same hospital fifteen years later, shuffling to the neurology suite along narrow corridors, yellowed peeling walls above shoe-scuffed skirting. The buzz of a fly caught in a striplight's flicker The blutak dots and torn curling posters. The sour smell of urine from the blocked toilet. I remember all this.

And I remember the words Parkinson's Disease casually stated. No build up, no drum roll. Just the simple sentence "You have Parkinson's disease. Any questions?" Although I have so many now, I had none then. I thanked the doctor for her time and that was that. The neurologist's door blew shut behind me.

I stood for a second listening to the wind rattling the door in its frame then drove back to work. Rather like police at an accident shepherding onlookers "Move along, there's nothing to see".

11th December 2006.

Funny, cos I don't usually remember dates.

November

Death and Drink

4th November 2009 ~ Drink!

Alcohol has many effects on the brain and nerve cells. It potentiates the effects of inhibitory amino acid neurotransmitters and reduces activity in the motor planning parts of the frontal cortex.

But by the most significant effect of alcohol is on the brain's exaggeration centre, that part of the brain so well developed among anglers. Trust me, I'm a scientist – I know this stuff.

Like a racehorse kept on a tight neuronal rein, the pop of a cork is the equivalent of a sharp spur to the exaggeration centre's soft flank. With the exaggeration centre at a trot, we become bold. Two glasses of cooking sherry and the stammering country vicar has become a voluble pillar of the General Synod. When the exaggeration centre breaks into a canter, boldness is replaced with heroics. Take Kevin, who once won a goldfish at a fair in Daventry, add a can or two of cider and suddenly he's Hemingway, catching swordfish in the sunset off Key West. Or Patrick, once flicked into a hedge by an angry heifer near Hereford. After a couple of Pinot Grigios, he's aching to show you where he was gored, running with the bulls in Pamplona.

Clippety clop. The only thing running is the exaggeration centre. We've all done it.

Alcohol loosens tongues, removes inhibitions and heightens our emotions. But this manifests itself in different ways in different people. Just like Parkinson's where some shake, some freeze and some stumble, alcohol's effects vary.

Which brings me to my friend Julius. A glass of wine turns this gentle tweed jacketed academic into a enthusiastic conversationalist, happy to talk about anything from soldering irons to Strauss waltzes. Fine. But an hour later and Julius has passed via gesticulating drink-spilling exuberance, then maudlin nostalgia, to a taciturn picture of glum introspection, tearfully hunched on the sofa. Bipolar, I'm sure of it.

Ham, my oldest friend – we have known each other for nigh on forty years – is the only man I know whose conversation is untouched by drink. Ham is the same avuncular host, whether sipping a small manzanilla at sunset or, five prandial hours later, after a hogshead of claret. Drink just doesn't touch him. By the end of an evening he is as coherent as ever. Unlike his guests. Any foolish enough to match him drink for drink have long since been zipped into body bags. Ham remains lucid. As does Meredith, his wife, two peas in a pod. They even live in a deconsecrated pub. So Ham can honestly say he spends all night at the pub.

But there you go, I'm exaggerating again. In fairness Ham just enjoys the finer things in life and shares that pleasure with his friends. But even Ham's patience can be tried. Buttonholed one evening at the bar of the Ass and Radiator, Ham studiously ignored the self-righteous braying until pressed directly "why do you feel the need to drink?" Ham took a lengthy draught of ale and turned to the source of his irritation. "To make you interesting" he growled.

My friend Rollo and I used to make dull drinks parties more interesting by slipping into an alter ego. For most of the mid eighties, I was Perseus Popadopolos, proud owner of a fleet of kebab vans on the North Circular. It was much more fun than being a postgraduate neuroscience student. And Rollo shed his life as a trainee barrister to become Reg Diamond, selling secondhand Skodas from a bombsite lot behind Catford High Street. He even had a sheepskin coat.

Well it was funny at the time.

Whether you are Julius or Ham, Rollo or Reg, Perseus or Meredith, all alcohol-fuelled behaviour comes down to actions on nerve cells, tickling those little synapses. Sadly, by the morning, the same synapses are more pickled than tickled.

Don't get me wrong – this is no sanctimonious spiel about the demon drink. Nor am I Oliver Reed, despite the odd youthful indiscretion. It's a part of growing up to learn that beers with names like Skullsplitter do exactly what it says on the tin.

But those days are passed. Whether due to advancing age or advancing Parkinson's, I find myself less thirsty than in my youth. No longer do I set about a bottle of fourteen percent Aussie Shiraz with the urgent fervour of a bee seeking nectar. Most evenings I can barely finish a glass. I sip where once I quaffed, tipple rather than gulp.

At the pub after a game of cricket, I commit a crime even worse than dropping a sitter – I leave some of my beer, like a child unable to finish their greens.

Thirst aside, there are more immediate issues. Like many fellow Parkies, I have a drinking problem – I just keep spilling the stuff. And perversely, this is in proportion to the significance of the drink. A fluted crystal glass full of Veuve Clicquot at a launch party will invariably be spilt. It is as though my internal Sat Nav has programmed the wrong destination: Safeway Soave – destination mouth, Pichon Longueville '61 – destination carpet, Oddbins Orvieto – mouth, Chateau D'Yquem '67 – shirtfront, wife's blouse and antique persian rug.

All of this is a far cry from the person who met his PD specialist for the first time three years ago to discuss medication. It had been a long consultation and I'm ashamed to say that one of my first questions was "Can I still have a drink?"

"Of course" he said "but you probably won't want to."

Now there's a sobering thought.

9th November 2009 ~ The hardest goodbye

Every day for a month, my brother, sister or I had driven with my father to the hospital to visit my mother. And every evening my father had phoned from the hospital with updates. Some better, some worse. Some verging on optimism, others brief and despondent. Yesterday, the phone rang as usual. But sometimes you just have a sense, and I knew before he spoke.

"Bad news I'm afraid" he said in a halting monotone. "We lost her this afternoon"

There are no words for this. Nothing that even begins to describe the desolation. No bitter similes, no dolorous metaphors to draw upon. No well-turned phrase nor hackneyed hyperbole. Nothing.

How do you say goodbye to your mother, the person who gave you life? Stop the clocks, turn pictures to the wall in the sombre rituals of death? Talk to her empty armchair and say all the things you should have said? Take comfort in the trivial, in mechanical daily routine? Busy yourself with the many arrangements?

And from this numbness, how should I remember her?

The mother who cuddled me, as a toddler, on her lap after my evening bath? The mother who washed my mouth out with soap when her eight year old son first swore aloud? The mother who bandaged my playground-scraped knees and dabbed away tears? The mother who turned heads, so often mistaken by strangers for Vivien Leigh? The mother who cried tears of joy when I walked up to collect my degree? The mother who cried tears of anger when I told her I had Parkinson's, railing at the injustice? The mother who still always had a smile for her children even when ravaged with arthritis and in that pain that morphine barely touches?

Even the mother who spent her last month in hospital, passed ignominiously from ward to ward as the doctors ran out of ideas?

A rollercoaster month of despair and hope. A month of phone calls and cards, of photographs and grandchildren. Of flowers, candles and prayers. Of glum drives to the hospital, my father and I lost in our thoughts. Of anonymous draughty corridors. Of times when she seemed to walk to the edge and peer over the precipice only to step back. Of nurses rallying to look after a former ward sister, with that special bond nurses have for their own kind. Of doctors talking coldly of 'procedures' and 'quality of life' and 'options'.

In the end, there were no options. She drifted away from us by degrees, lucid moments of sunshine increasingly obscured by clouds. Sometimes with us, sometimes withdrawn to another place. Monosyllabic mostly.

She knew things were bad and occasionally asked "Am I dying?"

Late one Thursday afternoon, tired and weakened by the day's scans and tests, she was briefly with us, aware of our fretful figures at the foot of her bed. Amid a spaghetti of tubes and wires, she looked from my father, to my brother, to me. A feeble smile and movement of the hand. A blessing almost.

"Handsome boys" she whispered slowly "My handsome boys."

16th November 2009 ~Art for art's sake

Grandma Bluedoor lived in Doncaster near the Town Fields in a small bungalow with – you've guessed – a blue front door. She called it Persian Blue, hinting at Arabian Nights giddy with cedarwood and incense. But Doncaster was no Samarkand and the flapping market day stalls outside the Black Bull were far from the Kasbah. On wintery Tuesday mornings, while my mother had her hair 'done' in town, a procedure lasting the best part of two hours, Grandma Bluedoor painted me and my sister. Sometimes we would play cards or talk by the gas fire in the living room, its quiet reassuring hiss filling any pauses. Other days I would just listen as she spoke of her childhood in Blackpool and Wigan. Or of the war, recalling the drone of bombers flying over her house at night on their way to Liverpool. The distant thunder of explosions and the terrible chimney red glow over the horizon as the docks took their nightly pounding. Like all artists, she could paint with words as well as brushes, chalks or pastels. Sometimes we painted together. She said I had a talent and encouraged my stumbling efforts at still life – wavy fruitbowls full of livid, misshapen apples and bananas like neon hockey sticks. But often she would paint, as I sat for long hours at the window in the 'front parlour' wistfully listening to my friends playing football outside. My grandmother bought my patience with promises of Lemon Sherbets, Love Hearts and Spangles.

All this art was wasted on me. Although comfortably the best artist in my class, I merely went through the motions, greeting each new assignment with petulant disinterest. Each term my school report gave me an A-, the A a grudging acknowledgement of ability, but qualified by a minus that spoke accusingly of squandered talent. I was used to As. In fact, I was pretty good at most subjects. Except science. So, with the kind of perverse logic common to adolescents, I became a scientist.

Art was for sissies. And girls. I threw my paintset in the bin with its little watercolour pots of Burnt Sienna, Vermilion, and Prussian Blue. Some sort of statement.

But, like Father Brown's unknowing penitent, caught with an unseen hook and a long invisible line, I would one day be brought to shore with 'a twitch upon the thread'.

I left science in 2003, three years before I was diagnosed with PD but already showing symptoms if I had only recognised them for what they were. But that's another story for another day. For a year I was out of work, a shuffling aimless figure filling my day in that Bermuda Triangle of coffee shop, library and post office.

On my way to the library one crisp autumn morning, my attention was drawn to a flyer advertising courses in stained glass art and design. I called the number, unsure what to say. A week later I was standing at an easel, holding a paintbrush in my hand for the first time in forty years. It felt like coming home.

It is sometimes said that artists are born not made, that you cannot create artists and it is useless to do so. That we are products of our nature not our nurture, the fruits of a great chromosomal waltz. The genetic blueprint that gives us blue eyes or brown hair is the same design that makes us scientists or artists, orchestra conductors or bus conductors. Our brains are wired at birth, like enormous telephone exchanges. Scary huh?

But imagine that it was not so, that we could create artists or maybe unmask latent talent, somehow fan the flickering embers of creativity.

OK, let's go further. Imagine that we knew the particular pathways through the brain responsible for creativity. The nerve bundles that made Gustav Klimt a painter, Alan Ginsberg a poet or Miles Davis a musician.

Sound far fetched? Well try this for size. Imagine that we could reduce creativity to a single molecule, one neurotransmitter that fans the flickering flame of creation. One card from the shuffled deck.

What if you could take a pill to boost creativity, to inspire you, to move those brushes over the canvas, to make the words flow onto the page or the notes float in the air?

What if I told you that I had taken those tablets, popped those very pills this morning?

Am I a junkie? Is this science fiction?

No. Er, that's no to both questions. There is just such a 'creativity pathway', its neurotransmitter is known and there are drugs that enhance its function. Bingo!

The nerve bundle in question is the mesolimbic pathway, a great trunk of neurones that passes like a motorway from the ventral tegmental area to the busy termini of the limbic forebrain – the nucleus accumbens, the olfactory tubercle and the frontal cortex. This powerhouse of creativity is fuelled by – cue the drum roll – dopamine. That's right, our old and much missed friend, the same dopamine that is so conspicuously AWOL from the corpus striatum.

Some of the drugs we take – the dopamine agonists – can affect this mesolimbic pathway. In the same way that they boost dopamine function in the striatum, they also increase traffic on the 'creativity highway'. The drugs have no sat nav. They are just as likely to find their way to the limbic forebrain as the striatum.

So what happens when you unleash a horde of dopamine agonists on an unsuspecting mesolimbic pathway? The same agonists welcomed like prodigal sons in the empty striatum, are given a more cautious reception in the bustling limbic forebrain. In the striatum, dopamine agonists are all pleases and thankyous while in the nucleus accumbens, they are storytelling braggards, flirting with your wife and daughter while drinking your best whisky. In the striatum, dopamine agonists fill a void. In the limbic system they muscle in and further excite already busy synapses.

Many people with Parkinson's (I am doing my best to be politically correct this week) find that their drugs open up vistas of creativity. The drugs that unlock frozen limbs also lubricate ossified imaginations. Ideas run riot. Painting, poetry, sculpture - you name it. All down to busier mesolimbic synapses.

And this remarkable surge of creativity is acknowledged in the annual Mervyn Peake Awards, at the World Parkinson's Congress, and in countless art groups up and down the country. Art and Parkinson's are like peaches and cream. We paint, we draw, we stitch, write, photograph and sculpt. And it's all down to those mesolimbic dopamine synapses, crackling and fizzing with activity.

But there is a price. In Parkinson's there's always a price. This same mesolimbic pathway is the one responsible for shopping, gambling and other darker behaviour. Too much dopamine and our creative urges spill over into chaos. Enthusiasm becomes anarchy. It's a fine balance. We would all like to be Van Gogh, the painter of starry nights and sunflowers. Few would want to become the later Van Gogh staring threateningly back at us with bandaged head and missing ear. That's the thing with dopamine – you can have too much of a good thing.

My eldest, Catherine, has plenty of dopamine. Her Art GCSE year was a riot of collage, paint, ink, gouache and paste and, for a year, Catherine's bedroom was awash with painting paraphernalia. Our cleaner despaired. I snapped.

"Catherine, your bedroom is a disgrace. Clean it now".

"I can't – it hasn't been marked yet"

"Marked? Your bedroom marked?"

"But it's not a bedroom. It's a mixed media installation"

Thank you Tracey Emin.

26th November 2009 ~ Shopping

Last Sunday I decided to nip out to the industrial estate to buy a new laptop. For a few weeks I had been eyeing up a mini netbook with more bells and whistles than a Morris Men's AGM. Bluetooth, wifi and goodness knows what else. By any standard, it was a mouthwatering bit of kit. I told the wife where I was going. "Oh, I'll come too" said Claire casually. "OK" I said "I didn't know you were interested in computers". An hour later we left Comet with a Hotpoint WMF720 with cold water feed and twin speed spin cycle.

Yes. A washing machine. Not a laptop.

The word "ambush" comes to mind.

"You're very quiet" said Claire as we got back in the car. The vein on my temple was throbbing. We drove home in silence.

"Who's Mr Grumpy today" says Claire.

And the laptop?

I am sorry but "Wait and see what Santa brings you" does not cut the mustard. Why couldn't Santa have bought the washing machine and let me buy the laptop,

I'd like to know. If I had been a five year old, I would have stamped my feet. Actually I did anyway.

But it's my own fault really. After all, this is not the first time that Claire has morphed my techie gadgets into white goods. Over the years, MP3 players have become microwave ovens, a new flat screen TV transforms into a fridge freezer, and digital cameras mysteriously are suddenly vacuum cleaners. No matter how exciting the gizmo, it somehow ends up as a fridge, electric hob, toaster or sandwich maker. Claire has previous.

This is a pattern repeated in thousands of families nationwide.

I ask you - is there are any more depressing sight than a husband gloomily traipsing around Curry's or Dixons while his wife compares all seventy eight tumble dryers? After the first five machines, even the rictus smile of feigned interest on hubbys's face has faded. Another ten and he is casually shuffling toward the video cameras whilst still remaining in earshot. After a further twenty dryers he has abandoned all pretence and is fast losing the will to live. Quarter of an hour later, the wife reaches a decision just as the husband finally reaches his own, coming down narrowly in favour of pills over a noose.

Taking the husband's credit card, the youth on the till asks earnestly "Will this product do everything you want?" What kind of question is that?

"It's only got to dry clothes" says the husband testily "it ought to be able to make a fist of that". The youth looks up from the till and immediately thinks better of asking whether they want the extended warranty.

Bad though this is, there are worse examples. Woe betide the fellow who decides to show his sensitive side, by 'helping' his fiancee shop for clothes. Six hours later he is sat alone, shellshocked, in the Fool and Firkin. How could his helpful advice have somehow broken off the engagement? And where did she learn those words?

For men, mixed shopping is like juggling dynamite. You just know that sooner or later you will slip up with too candid an assessment. If you are asked for an "honest" opinion on whether a blouse suits the wearer, think long and hard before actually venturing an honest opinion. If you must be truthful, at least do so in the most imprecise and vague circumlocution possible.

And don't even think about cracking a joke.

Mind you, hesitation is just as bad. Fulsome praise, delivered a split second late, is equally damning. "You don't like it. I can tell"

Even with years of training and experience, some situations still always lead to casualties. "What do you think of these two frocks?" is a hospital pass. There is no right answer. Sinking to the ground clutching your chest, Fawlty style, is probably worth a shot.

To be perfectly honest, men and women should shop separately. They have different objectives and methods. It's that old hunter-gatherer thing.

Male shopping is focussed and functional. Rechargeable batteries, beer, hacksaw. Fifteen minutes tops.

Female shopping is an entirely different beast. A coterie of friends trawling Covent Garden for designer shoes, jewellery, nails and Belgian chocolates. Like locusts with credit cards. To a man – well, to me at least – this is less a day's entertainment than a Dantean vision of Purgatory.

All of which leads me on to the subject of Parkinson's and shopping. Let's face it, this is a touchy subject. If you believe the tabloids, our medicines turn us all into shopaholics unable to resist a bargain. We stop shaking and start shopping. "Buy one get one free", "Fifty percent off", "Everything must go". These are green lights to the Parkie shopper. Apparently, we cannot be trusted with credit cards and think nothing of remortgaging the house to fuel our shopping sprees, leaving our families destitute.

Sound familiar? I thought not. Maybe just a tiny flicker of recognition?

Let's talk turkey.

I should be careful what I say here because I don't want to trivialise this or make fun. And I don't want to scare you either. But, that aside, this is a genuine issue for some of us. It seems to be less the Parkinson's than a combination of certain personality traits and drug treatments. But which?

The main trait is impulsivity, those unplanned actions made without thought of consequence. That's mostly risk taking to you and I. Ask yourself - are you the kind of person who drives below the speed limit and will only overtake when the road is empty for a mile ahead. Or do you weave in and out of traffic and overtake on blind bends, pitting your driving skills against the likelihood of a car coming the other way? It's probably no surprise that a sensation-seeking extrovert is more at risk of shopping frenzy than a timid introvert.

And the drugs? Mostly the finger seems to point at the dopamine agonists. Not to any individual drug, more the class itself. Certainly that's the view of the tabloids.

But let's be absolutely clear – these are generalities. Not every bunjee-jumping, fire-eating stuntman on handfuls of dopamine agonist will flog the house to pay for his scratchcard habit. Nor should the quiet mousy librarian, agonising over that second digestive, think he's automatically in the clear. Just be aware.

What about me – my patches constantly drip feed me with my dopamine agonist. Do I hear voices saying buy this, buy that? Do I constantly feel a pressing need for a new DVD player?

Not at all.

Besides, we have a new washing machine already. Bought it last Sunday.

December

Hassim and the Emu

6th December 2009 ~ Spam

Wednesdays. It may be long ago but I'm sure it was always Wednesdays.

It couldn't have been Monday. My father had evening surgery so Monday evenings were always something easy like baked beans or cheese on toast. Tuesday was generally a mess of leftovers – the reheated remnants of the Sunday roast, plated and warmed in the oven. If after-school football ran late, the leftovers were dried, almost mummified. Often recollection of the previous Sunday lunch was the only way of identifying Tuesday's supper – the culinary equivalent of using dental records

But Wednesdays were Spam fritters. Slices of Spam a centimetre thick – that's nearly half an inch in old money - deep fried. And when I say deep fried, I mean deep. Deep as Louis Armstrong singing What a Wonderful World. That deep. On the stove rested a gigantic pan full of sunflower oil. I used to tell my mother it was a cauldron. "Then what does that make me?" she would ask, pretending to be hurt. But pan or cauldron, it was home to about two gallons of oil that would gradually be brought up to a temperature close to the earth's core. meanwhile, my mother would dip coat the Spam in batter and sidle nervously up to the cauldron. At arm's length, she flipped the fritters into the pan and, with a squeal, turned tail. Once satisfied that there was to be no conflagration, she would emerge from behind the kitchen counter and return to shelling peas, even humming nonchalantly to herself while Stromboli bubbled and spat behind her.

After Monday's and Tuesday's monochrome austerity, the humble Spam fritter was food in Technicolour. With a blat of ketchup on top, they made homework bearable. Even quadratic equations. When there were chips too, I was sure I had died and gone to Heaven. In the same way that Spam filled the bellies of postwar Britain, still rumbling under the shadow of rationing, so the Spam fritter ended the post-weekend deprivation in the Stamford family. Celebration time. I even have visions of marching bands and ticker tape. They were that good.

There is, I have discovered, a Spam website. No, really. And even – I'm not making this up – a Spam fanclub. With a newsletter. Best of all, if you join, they send you a card on your birthday! You know, I can't prove it but I bet they have secret handshake too.

If I am honest, I have not eaten Spam since I was a child. It now seems to belong in another time, like Dandelion and Burdock, corned beef and bags of crisps with tiny blue screws of salt. Yes, I know we can still buy most of these. We just don't, that's all.

Nowadays spam, albeit with a small "s", means something quite different. Mention 'spam' to anyone now and they won't be thinking of processed meat, that's for sure.

Spam is now synonymous with junk mail, the electronic equivalent, if you will, of all those flyers for pizza delivery, gutter clearance or cheap MOTs. Mostly it's harmless or absurd.

If I believed everything I read in the email spam folder, the outlook would be rather mixed. And confusing. Apparently my bank account has been suspended and needs reactivation with all my personal details and passwords. And my credit card password needs to be verifed online because of "suspected fraudulent activity". But it's not all bad – I get any number of hot stockmarket tips – Abyssinian zinc, Moldovan asbestos, you name it.

And medicines – treatments for everything from flatulence and halitosis to advanced cancer and Parkinson's. All derived from a rare Namibian tree fungus known only to five people. This technology does not come cheap, so I am terribly lucky to have such a unique opportunity to invest. It says so here.

Then there are the miracle diets and cosmetic surgeons. No sooner has one email arrived offering to take six inches off my waistline than another proposes to do the exact opposite to my dangly bits.

Then I had a charming letter from a Mr Dibango in Burkina Faso about some $50 billion he was keen to move into my bank account if I could help him out with legal fees of a few thousand pounds or some such bagatelle. I'd love to help Mr D but, as I said, my bank account is frozen. Another time perhaps.

And a nice Chinese chappie has offered me (and a million others) the chance to buy a fake Rolex. Mr Dong must be quite an entrepreneur because he also sells Viagra and wants to introduce me to a rather fetching young Ukrainian lady who can't seem to buy soap in her country. Apparently Ludmilla is a "very dirty girl". Poor thing.

Anyway, I am busy buying suntan lotion and swimming trunks – It seems I have won a holiday in the Seychelles and just need to send the "administration fee", a small matter of £300, to a PO Box in Bootle. Perhaps I could sell some of my shares in that porcine aviation company. I understand they are having a bit of a hiccup so my stock certificate is delayed.

Just as I finish my packing, two more emails arrive – one is from a language school, teaching Inglish to foreigners. The other is from Mr Dong offering me tickets for Glyndebourne at £600 each.

I suppose I could always take Ludmilla, if she has had a chance to freshen up a bit.

13th December 2009 ~ Bedtime story

I want to tell you a story. Dim the lights and find make yourself cosy. Are you sitting comfortably? Then I'll begin

Many years ago, a rich merchant in Baghdad sent his servant Hassim to the marketplace to buy provisions - some dates, oil, bread and wine. The sun shone brightly among the palm trees and the merchant did not mind that Hassim would often stop and play chess or drink coffee with friends before returning.

Hassim was not long gone when the merchant heard a muffled sound from the cellar. He called out from the top of the stone steps "Hassim? Is that you Hassim?"

He lit a torch, and in its oily smoke, saw the ashen face of his servant, cowering breathless among the oil jars."

What is the matter Hassim" he asked" how long have you been here?"

Hassim shook but said nothing. The merchant clapped his hands. Farah the housekeeper appeared. "A drink for Hassim" said the merchant "Fetch wine".

"Hassim you are frightened." he said "What has frightened you my friend? Did you lose the money at the chess table? Have you been robbed?"

The merchant paused "It is a beautiful day and you have no business to be so frightened. Come my friend, tell me"

He held out an earthenware beaker of wine.

Hassim looked back and blinked. A mouse, scurrying among the grain baskets made him start. The beaker fell to the floor and broke.

The merchant handed Hassim his own beaker. Hassim looked up and their eyes met briefly. The servant gulped at the wine and felt its warming course. The master sat down beside him and for a moment they were old friends not master and servant. The merchant smiled.

"Master, I must leave you" he spluttered, as panic gripped him again "I must go now. I can't wait. I'm in danger".

"There is no danger here" said the merchant. "This is my house and you are safe from whatever has frightened you".

"No master, I must leave. He knows where I live and he will find me here. You cannot protect me".

"I am a man of power and we have guards. There is nothing to be afraid of".

"Master" said Hassim "if you had a thousand guards you could not protect me from him".

"From whom? Baghdad is your city" said the merchant "You have no enemies here".

"Master I went to the market as you asked this morning. I bought dates. I bought bread and wine. The market was crowded as usual and I looked for Ali to play chess. On the far side of the market I thought I saw him and called out. He turned and as he did so I noticed his hands, hands of a corpse.

Hassim shook and gulped the wine.

"He raised his arm and pointed to me. And as he did so, his *keffiyeh* fell away and I saw his face".

Hassim shuddered violently. "I must get away now. I cannot delay. He will find me here".

The merchant held Hassim's shoulders. "Be calm" he said.

"But you don't understand master, it was the face of death. The empty sockets, the skin dry and thin like papyrus, the teeth blackened and broken".

Hassim screwed his eyes closed against the image. In a faltering voice he said slowly "he made a grimace. He was threatening me".

Hassim gasped for breath. "He will come for me here. He knows. He will come here tonight. I have to leave now".

"Master, I need a camel to take me away so he will not find me. I have saved money. I have shekels. Let me buy a camel, master to take me away from here".

"Hassim" said the merchant gently shaking his servant "this is madness. Come. See".

He helped Hassim to his feet "Death is not here. See the goats suckling their young. See the lizards basking in the sun. This is life. Death is not here".

"But he will come tonight. If I am here he will come for me". Hassim ran upstairs and returned with a carved wooden box. With a clatter the shekels fell to the floor.

"Take them master. I must have a camel. I beg you".

He fell at the merchant's feet.

"Hassim, get up" said the merchant. "Have I not shown you that you are safe here?". Before Hassim could say anything, he held his hand up.

"I see not". he sighed. There was a pause.

"Then you shall have my best arab stallion".

"But I cannot buy the stallion, master".

"Nor shall you. Hassim take the stallion. Ride to Samarra in the north. I have friends there and they will take you in. They will look after you. When you are ready, return to me and I will greet you with open arms. In a day, a month or a year".

The merchant watched, eyes screwed tight as Hassim beecame a dusty speck near the horizon. Samarra was a hundred miles to the north. Even at this gallop, he would not be there before nightfall.

"God's speed, my friend" said the merchant under his breath, "God's speed".

As the merchant turned away, a thought crossed his mind. "I am a man of standing, a man of power. I will not have my servant frightened. I will not have Hassim threatened by anybody. Of this world or the next. I will seek Death out and talk to him".

The merchant called for his carriage and rode to the marketplace. The sun, overhead, beat down from a cloudless sky and the merchant wiped his brow.

The market was all but over. A few stalls lingered among the baked sand. The air was heavy with incense, overripe fruit and meats roasting on skewers. In the far corner Hassim's friend Ali played chess and pulled on a *hookah*.

The merchant looked left and right, up and down, near and far. Two tethered goats bleated. Death was nowhere.

He took a seat near Ali. Head in his hands, he glumly called for dates and a glass of *raki*. He was hot and his journey was fruitless. He thought of Hassim, driven by his fear, galloping across the desert to avoid death. Here he was seeking death but unable to find him.

"Thank you" he said as the dates were placed in front of him. Only when the *raki* was poured did he notice the bony hand. Startled, he looked up and, in an instant, found what he sought in the sightless eyes. He jumped up, knocking over the *raki* and dates.

As the flow of *raki* slowed t o a drip, he stood face to face with Death. He felt his chest rise and fall and his heart pound. The flies stopped buzzing. Somewhere a dog barked.

"Why?" he asked.

Death leant forward and the merchant felt his cold breath as he spoke softly.

"Explain"

"This morning my servant Hassim came to the market and you pointed at him and grimaced. You terrified him. Why?"

Death smiled. "I did not mean to frighten him" he said "nor did I grimace at him. My expression was one of surprise"

"Surprise?" said the merchant.

"Yes. I was surprised to see him here in Baghdad" said Death "for I have an appointment with him tonight in Samara".

NOTE: This is my retelling of "Appointment in Samarra" a short story by W. Somerset Maugham. Maugham's version itself is a retelling of a far older version, recorded in the Babylonian Talmud, Sukkah 53a

20th December 2009 ~ Christmas Past

I'm old enough to remember white Christmases. More to the point I'm old enough to remember when Christmases, or at least the Christmas holiday, seemed generally white. Every garden had its own snowman with pointy carrot nose and two lumps of coal for eyes. Nowadays I don't even know where you go to buy coal. Strange really considering that my grandfather was a coal merchant. He wouldn't be impressed.

To a child, Christmas meant snow. I was eight before I realised 'white Christmas' was two words not one, so inseparable were they. To a fifty two year old man with Parkinson's, snow means slips and falls, broken bones and visits to casualty. Snow compounds unsteadiness, makes faltering footsteps less confident. Snow hides cracks in the pavement loose paving and many other hazards. I no longer see snow but accidents. Wonder is replaced by a fear. Heavy snowfalls do not turn Northampton into Narnia.

But I digress. Back to Christmas and a snowy 1960s Doncaster

We lived in a tall Victorian terrace house on Thorne Road. In the living room was the biggest Christmas tree imaginable. Every year we insisted my father bought a bigger tree than the previous year. And every year he wrestled it up the stairs to our living room (the ground floor of the house was occupied by my father's surgery). More than once I would emerge from my bedroom to be confronted by what appeared to be a Norwegian forest making its way up the stairs towards me. It was like a scene from Macbeth. Only the continuo of muttering and oaths from my father behind it reassured me that the tree was not approaching under its own steam.

By the time the tree was in the living room, the wallpaper was torn, lampshades were askew, and pine needles littered the landing like hypodermics in a crack den. Everything in the house smelt of pine. Except for my father who smelt as though he'd gone fifteen rounds with Joe Bugner. But this did not distract him from the lights. It goes without saying they didn't work. For the next hour my father would be changing bulb after bulb in methodical sequence while Venetia and I made paper chains and Charlie gurgled in amusement from his high chair. Finally father declared the lights ready, and with a fanfare plugged them in, plunging the entire house instantly into darkness. Sometimes the neighbours too. The fuse box was in the basement and it would be another fifteen minutes before we had lighting again. My sister and I amused ourselves by playing murder in the dark while mother would decamp to the kitchen with a candle and a bottle of Bristol Cream until the 'all clear'.

Christmas Eve was always a slow crescendo of excitement. There was no school, no relatives to visit, and my father did not have surgery. Christmas Eve was family alone. Around late afternoon we had brief visits from some of my father's grateful patients – Mrs Ferruzzi with Grappa and panettone and bear hugs for my father. And Mr Kowalski, a retired Polish miner with bottles of Polish vodka. Every year. They were as much a part of Christmas as tinsel and baubles.

Less welcome were the local ruffians masquerading as carol singers who thought that a couple of growled lines of Jingle Bells entitled them to a the equivalent of a city banker's annual bonus. You didn't have to pay them of course. But finding the doorway used as a urinal was even less attractive. My father's solution was to close the blackout curtains and wait in an upstairs window with a powerful semiautomatic Russian assault rifle. Yes, I am joking – but he certainly felt that way. In any case, you couldn't get the ammunition in Doncaster.

A s night fell, and mother busied herself in the kitchen, my sister and I would watch the snow falling outside our window in big heavy flakes - the street outside silent but for the occasional swish of tyres or giggling revellers gingerly making their way home from The Salutation past the Gaumont cinema and Christ Church with its stained glass windows like beacons in the night. Muffled snatches of evensong broke the silence as the snow shrouded the headstones in the churchyard, falling on the quick and the dead alike.

By nine, my father would abandon his vigil, pack away the AK47, and pour himself a sherry.

The house smelt of Christmas. Cloves, citrus, brandy and cinnamon mingled with sausages and gravy as my mother cooked what she could before Christmas day itself. Usually we had a frozen turkey for Christmas and my mother started defrosting the fowl around October, or so it seemed. One year, at my mother's suggestion, my father bought a turkey from a local farm, freshly killed and plucked in front of him. It was the size of an emu and the farmer was ill-prepared for the stiff resistance the bird put up. For several minutes It was touch and go who would kill who. My father placed it on the dining room table with a thud, simultaneously striking a pose, hands on hips, like some latter day Nimrod.

We had a small turkey for Christmas dinner that year – nobody had thought to check whether the emu would fit in the oven.

Of course, the larger the turkey the longer it lasted. Turkey slices in a Boxing Day cold collation was one thing. Counting the New Year in with a festive turkey risotto was quite another. And turkey haggis on Burns night was a bridge too far, something nobody should have to face. My father – because that's what fathers do – ate the stringy bits we children would not. He hated waste. Still does. I have an enduring memory of him at the kitchen table staring glumly at a turkey sandwich like a figure from Conrad. "The horror, the horror" he seemed to be saying.

Around eleven, we children were despatched to bed, on the understanding that Father Christmas would not stop at houses where children were awake. On a small table on the landing was a carrot for the reindeer and a mince pie and thimble of sherry for Santa. One particularly fraught Christmas, Santa had a tumbler of whisky waiting for him. "But Santa will go all giggly" I said to mother. "Santa needs to" she replied.

I was usually the first to wake on Christmas morning and would tiptoe downstairs to establish that Santa had left presents. Even more impressive was the fact that he had successfully negotiated the holly I had packed into the chimney breast as a prank.

We children were under strict instructions from mother not to open anything until a parent was present. Naturally we paid no attention. Ten minutes after waking, everything was unwrapped and Charlie gurgled away from beneath a mountain of wrapping paper. One of us knocked over a plant pot.

The noise woke my parents. There was a moment before the full import dawned on them. Mother shrieked. "Dear God, they're in the living room". Both ran downstairs but it was too late - neither my sister nor I knew what belonged to who, nor who indeed had sent what. "Don't move" said mother as they tried to piece together the crime scene and ascribe the right donor to the correct gift and its intended recipient.

A period of comparative peace ensued as I played with my Thunderbird 2 and my sister decorated her dolls house in the style of Jackson Pollock with a tin of red emulsion she had found in the basement. The emulsion also added a new dimension of realism when my Action Man 'went postal' and machine gunned Sindy and her coterie of dolls. Fortunately my new tank had not come with batteries or things would have been worse.

When Christmas dinner was ready, mother rang a cowbell we had bought from Kuhtai and we descended like wolves on the dining room. My father heightened anticipation with a theatrically languid sharpening of the carving knife before he nodded and the turkey was wheeled in on a groaning trolley. While father carved, we pulled crackers and tickled Charlie. The jokes seemed worse each year but somehow we never tired of the compasses, keyrings, bottle openers, and whistles. The flaming of the Christmas pudding was always a treat. Steeped in brandy, the pudding lit with a ferocity that singed eyebrows. The ensuing laughter helped blunt the pain from teeth cracked by the many coins lurking within.

After dinner we watched the telly – a brooding mahogany edifice like a sideboard. Nestling like an eyeball in the centre of this structure, and perhaps no bigger than a dinner plate, was the screen. Bracketing the screen in stark contrast were huge speakers covered in a sort of green baize with an art deco sunset motif. Baize was appropriate since each speaker was the size of a snooker table. It had taken four men just to get it up the stairs.

Switching on the telly for the Queen's speech visibly dimmed the lights. That's if it didn't blow the fuses again. You could boil an egg in the time it took to warm up. Meanwhile, my sister and I hid round the back watching the glow from valves the size of marrows, and doubtless receiving doses of X rays normally reserved for radiotherapy. This thing fogged film

The day ended the same way each year – parents replete in postprandial torpor, children snorkelling their way through the Quality Street and Tizer. Tucked up in bed I asked my mother how Santa knew I liked my new toys.

"He knows" she said "he just knows".

28th December 2009 ~ Christmas Present

Christmas 2009 does not start well. Until five days before Christmas, Chateau Stamford is the house with no cheer. While the rest of the street is a fairy grotto of lights, rippling, pulsing and flickering in epileptiform abandon, our house is in near darkness. No winged reindeer, no inflatable Santas, no laughing snowmen. Our house stands resolutely apart like a semidetached Bates Motel. Children cross the street, dogs whimper, postmen will not walk up the drive.

All because of a face-off between parents and children. Wearied by the shocking state of disarray in their rooms, I tell the kids at the start of Advent that there will be no tree, decorations or lights until their rooms are tidy. A decade ago, this would have sent them scuttling upstairs like crabs to address the matter in a state of near panic. Not now. "Whatever" says Alice with the kind of contemptuous shrug only a sixteen year old girl can manage. So, for a fortnight, we wait to see who will blink first.

Inevitably it is me. In my usual abject parental capitulation, I wave the white flag five days before Christmas. The terms of surrender are as punitive as the Treaty of Versailles – the kids are prepared to decorate the tree and string up the lights if (and only if) I go up the steep ladder into an arctic loft to retrieve the baubles from among the dark chilly chaos of boxes and mouse traps while they play on the Wii. Half an hour later I emerge from the loft, blinking in the light, frozen to the core and shaking mouse droppings from my slippers. Claire meets me with a glass of mulled wine and a lecture about being too much of a soft touch.

This Christmas, as usual, we find ourselves on our knees seeking Jesus. Usually he is down the back of the sofa or stuck in a heating vent. Sometimes the son of God is in the vacuum cleaner among the tinsel. It doesn't matter where we put the crib each year, baby Jesus always goes AWOL. And it's always Him. Never something expendable or replaceable - at a pinch you could always shed a shepherd or one of the supporting cast of animals. But not Jesus. The Boss. Let's face it a nativity scene without the Big Guy doesn't really work. So I'm keeping a close eye on Jesus this year. It's electronic tagging next if the Messiah does a runner again.

On Christmas Eve, we play Scrabble. To add interest I offer to cook the Christmas dinner if I lose. I am on safe ground here because I hardly ever lose. As the letters run out, my word DINNER takes me 94 points clear of Claire. Job done. I pour myself a congratulatory glass of port as Claire stares with furrowed brow at her letters. Suddenly from nowhere she places SQUEEZED across a triple word square, even turning my carelessly placed D against me. 131 points and victory. Pandemonium breaks out with Claire and the girls all whoops and high fives as my Christmas dissolves in a hailstorm of sprouts. As Claire circles the living room on a victory lap, Alex puts his arm around me. "Never mind Dad" he says "just do pizza"

So disorientated am I by this linguistic setback that I forget to leave out the customary glass of sherry for Santa before going to bed.

I wake to the sound of Santa berating me about the sherry. I politely suggest that Santa had already drunk so many Snowballs that a sherry was superfluous.

We open presents. No orgiastic frenzy of ribbon and wrapping paper. With teenagers now, those days are past. Do you know, I rather miss setting up a video camera to catch the presents being unwrapped and prevent the kind of creative anarchy we inflicted on our parents. If Alex was unsure who sent the scale model Bugatti Veyron, we just replayed the tape. Obvious.

Claire and I start the day with Buck's Fizz. Unnoticed in the music room, our dog Flora starts her Christmas day with a box of liqueur chocolates, carelessly left beneath the tree. Grand Marnier, Cointreau, cherry brandy, whisky - all gone. Along with wrappers. Strangely she ignores the Drambuie. After a skinful of spirits, Flora can match me for unsteadiness as she thuds into the sofa.

But it's Christmas day – buoyed by a second glass of Buck's Fizz, I am not even worried about cooking Christmas dinner. Fear has no meaning for me (I have teenage daughters remember). Like a zen master, I enter the kitchen. Today I will show what calm efficiency can achieve. Claire decides to watch the zen master at work. No pressure. I pour a third Buck's Fizz and run through my list of required ingredients and timings.

Half the ingredients are missing.

"And the turkey should have been in the oven an hour ago" says Claire.

"Technically it was" I reply, glossing over the fact that I had omitted to switch the oven on.

Alice runs into the kitchen. The dog has been sick.

Suddenly, Christmas dinner begins to unravel. I weigh up my options. Do I swallow my pride and plead for assistance? Or serve an undercooked meal and poison the entire family. Claire reads the panic in my eyes and takes over. "You owe me." she says "Bigtime." "Can I do something?" I ask, now reduced to sous-chef. "Yes" she replies "ask Catherine to come and help". This is the culinary equivalent of having your epaulettes torn off and your sword snapped in half. Short of a letter in the Times, there can be no greater kitchen humiliation. The doorbell rings. I am half expecting Gordon Ramsay to compound my discomfiture but it turns out to be a neighbour borrowing eggs.

I pour myself another Buck's fizz and flick through the TV channels. Even Ant and Dec seem amusing. I mention this to Alice. "It's your medication" she says.

Christmas presents opened, the family busies itself with important jobs. Alex is inserting AAs into a radio-controlled Porsche. Alice is applying another coat of fluorescent nail varnish and Catherine is spending her iTunes voucher. Flora is in her basket sleeping off the mother of all hangovers. Claire is in the kitchen. 'nuff said.

My fourth Buck's Fizz sends me soundly to sleep. Alcohol and Azilect - top cocktail. I dream fitfully of being chased through a forest by hamsters the size of timber wolves. Just as the hamsters catch me, I am woken by Catherine.

"Were you dreaming?" she asks

"Hamsters" I blurt.

"Aww sweet"

January

Dogs and Driving

4th January 2010 ~ Christmas Future

Part of the fascination of the future is the unpredictable nature of the journey, the horizon obscured by bends in the road. Around every corner are surprises, often happy sometimes not. For many, the response to this uncertainty lies in planning for every eventuality. We create an illusion of control by our detailed mapping of possibilities. Others greet the vagaries of life with a fatalistic nonchalance, finding equal reassurance in the calm unfolding of events over which we hold no dominion.

Parkinson's changes your future in every way. To paraphrase Tom Isaacs, we are all somehow reconciled to living lives less wonderful than we had once imagined for ourselves. Our lives have past and present tenses but, like some tricky Latin verb, we struggle to see a cogent future. The horizon is even more hidden. Where there were bends in the road before, now there are hairpins. And its dark. And foggy. And the road is icy.

My point is this – you still make the journey but you will need the snow chains, fog lights and de-icer. We still make our own journey, rattling along slowly with our pills and potions.

Many of us believe we want to know the future. Many others would rather not. Some of us see our future in the hunched, broken figures at the Neurology outpatients. Some of us see it in the Marathon runners vigorously pushing back against the disease's course. For some of us, our days are marked by small victories, tiny triumphs in this endless war.

I can no more predict the future than anyone. But let's be clear: We can choose to be diminished or defined by this condition. We can let it lead or make it follow.

In A Christmas Carol, Scrooge asks of the phantom "You are about to show me shadows of the things that have not happened, but will happen in the time before us. Is that so, Spirit?"

The spirit says nothing but takes Scrooge off to see the future.

Suddenly I am Scrooge and we are flying over a snowy Yorkshire, the sun glinting off frozen ponds. Steam rises from roofs and smoke from chimneys. There's my parents' house in Doncaster. I can hear laughter. My sister and I are playing in the snow outside while my brother giggles in his pram. I can see my mother waving to my childhood self from the kitchen window. My father is dragging a Christmas tree to the front door.

We fly on south, weaving between clouds as we follow the A1. As afternoon becomes evening, the road becomes a river of light. We follow the M25 round to the east soaring over the Dartford bridge and past the navigation lights of the refineries. I swear I can hear the strains of 'Walking in the air'. The winter constellations Orion and Gemini seem brighter than ever. On we go over the rooftops of Kent, the Medway far below. There is my house. In the garden is the last of the snow crocodile Catherine and her friend made last week. Alice is playing with the dog while Alex and his friend Tom are on the Wii. Claire and I are staggering back from dinner with Anton and Freia, reeling under the influence of Freia's sloe gin.

Again we swoop through the clouds and suddenly it is day. The landscape is familiar but somehow different. It is our house but with a big conservatory. I recognise Claire in the kitchen with Freia. A young man cheers loudly – I realise it is Alex, watching the cricket on the television. He must be in his twenties. I see Catherine playing the flute. Alice is wearing jodhpurs. Claire picks up a crying baby. Whose? The newspaper, unnoticed on the doormat, says 24th December 2020.

The house is full of guests, girlfriends and boyfriends. But I am nowhere. The spirit and I walk unseen among them, catching snatches of conversation. Freia offers Catherine a glass of something deep purple "Your dad used to love my blackberry whisky" I hear her say. "Dad wrote this poem when I was seventeen" says Catherine. Alex calls Tom to watch another Aussie wicket fall "That's how Dad used to get out – always playing across the line". They laugh. The radio is playing *O Mio Babbino Caro*. "Dad would have liked this" says Alice "cricket and Puccini!". Freia and Claire are handing round glasses of champagne. Anton is making a speech, struggling to make himself heard over the din. His voice fades in and out like a poorly tuned radio "Friends and family ....an empty place ..... sorely missed at Christmas ..... unexpected turn of events.....coping today without Jon"

I turn to the phantom. I want to speak but he gestures me to be quiet.

The phone rings. "Yes.... No.....Ok....fine" I hear Catherine say

"Who is it?" asks Claire

"It's Dad" says Catherine "He got the earlier flight home from the meeting. He'll be here in half an hour"

11th January 2010 ~ Cracking the Code

We Parkies see the inside of hospitals often enough. Too often if you ask me. Whether shivering and quivering in Outpatients or splayed out in traction like a plaster starfish after tripping on a loose paving slab, we are there. We have front row seats for the drama and bustle of the hospital, with nurses weaving from ward to ward in cheerful choreography, a ballet of bedpans, a symphony of stethoscopes. And all our lives are recorded in disarming detail in the patient notes.

I ask you, how many times has your neurologist opened your notes with the flamboyance of a conductor about to address a Beethoven overture? Just like a musical score, the notes re a mass of coded comments, medical shorthand and elusive acronyms. He makes sense of them and assumes we don't.

Ever wondered what those hieroglyphs actually mean?

In years gone by, hospital notes were confidential and physicians wrote what they pleased about the patients in their care. Sometimes, purely on clinical grounds you understand, they might be a tad fulsome in their assessment of a pretty young lady's attributes. Or, just very occasionally, and purely motivated by the need to have a full clinical picture, they could be a mite derogatory about a patient's cranial capacity.

But the new health service glasnost meant that we, the patients (or are we customers now?) could rummage through our notes whenever we wanted. So the physician, made mindful of litigation, used code to outline our failings and foibles. Mr Bloggs was now Dys-synaptogenic rather than just plain stupid. And his gum chewing peroxide blond daughter was no longer an airhead – she had Acute Pneumoencephalopathy. Geddit?

Necessity is the mother of invention so a whole lexicon of phrases and acronyms evolved to fill this need with the kind of black humour beloved of the caring professions. Nothing was going to cramp their style.

An anxious patient becoming overwrought by a perceived delay in treatment is a D.Q. with an A.H.F. (Drama Queen having an Acute Hissy Fit). Left in a side room to cool off, they quickly become a Buzzer Junkie (a patient who pressed the call button for no good reason). Some of these are Frequent Flyers (patients who spend more time in A&E than the staff). When there is nothing wrong with them the notes say D.I.F.F.C. - Dropped In For Friendly Chat. If repeated attempts to persuade the patient they are healthy fall on deaf ears, a note in the margin of S.Y.B. (Save Your Breath) makes the point with a curt elegance.

In any case doctors are overworked and underpaid. OK maybe not the latter. Besides, a busy A&E is no place to listen to an organ recital (a hypochondriac's medical history). Casualty iss bursting with organ donors (motorcyclists) or Ralphie McYakkers (young drunks vomiting), punctuated by the odd F.T.F. - Failed to Fly (botched suicide attempt). It's even worse on the D&D - Death and Doughnuts (night shift) where most admissions are A.A.L.F.D.s – Another Objectionable Person Looking For Drugs (think it through). Some patients are completely Dagenham (3 stops beyond Barking on the District line) and an aggressive disturbed patient (a Father Jack) often finds his treatment options limited to the disquieting B-52 (combined 5mg of Haloperidol + 2mg of Ativan) which lends new meaning to the term carpet bombing.

Otherwise it was just O.A.P.s (OverAnxious Parents) bringing kids with Spots 'n' Dots (the usual childhood fevers - measles, mumps, and chicken pox). A course of Bug Juice (antibiotics) usually does the trick.

It is just the same in the operating theatres. A Foreverectomy (operation that lasted a very long time) is testing for patients and sturgeons (surgeons) alike and when the surgeon calls for 6 bottles of the House Red in the middle of a complex procedure, it is rarely a cause for celebration. Some patients had so many operations they had Zorro Belly or Tube Map Tum. But don't lose heart - you could be treated to The Toaster (defibrillator). Late afternoon cases are Hit and Runs (quick operations in order to be at the other kind of theatre before the curtain rises). But however quickly the surgery is done, you don't want to find the surgeon had Buried the Hatchet (left a surgical instrument inside a patient) when the patient is wheeled back to Expensive (Intensive) Care. Back in ICU, patients are usually Eating In (receiving intravenous feeding). Especially those who have scored a Hat Trick (patient with 3 tubes into him).

Of course diagnosis is the real key to medicine and medical students quickly learn to blag their way with confident acronyms. It is easy if they are presented with a Janitor's fracture - a fracture so obvious that a janitor (cleaner) could diagnose it. But if symptoms are misleading, this amounts to a clear case of Fallaciopisces rufus (red herring). When really stumped for a diagnosis, G.O.K. (God Only Knows) or D.1.1.K. (Damned if I know) are as good an admission of defeat as any. Above all, medical students try to deliver a diagnosis without a podo-oral insertion (foot in mouth). And if they do make a mess of it there is always the chance to diagnose S.O.D.D.I. (Some Other Doctor Did It). When treatment options are exhausted there was always T.E.E.T.H. - Tried Everything Else, Try Homeopathy. For particularly troubling cases, the notes may say D.T.M.A. (Don't Transfer to Me Again).

When things are turning out badly the notes read J.I.C. (Jesus is calling) or G.R.A.F.O.B. (Grim Reaper at Foot of Bed). But be reassured: patients don't actually die – instead they are moved to the 10th floor (in a 9 storey hospital) or they might A.R.T. (Approach Room Temperature). Sometimes patients are transferred to the E.C.U. (Eternal Care Unit). Even so, some very sick patients still beat the odds (Coffin Dodgers).

Sadly most of this vocabulary is no longer used. And I think medicine is all the poorer for it.

My favourite acronym?

P.R.A.T.F.O. - Patient Reassured And Told to Go Away

17th January 2010 ~ Pets

Let me introduce Flora. Flora is a seven year old white standard poodle we have had since she was a puppy. But she is so much more than that. Flora is perhaps my main weapon in the fight against Parkinson's. We all know that exercise is important in Parkinson's and helps put the brakes on the disease's progress. Flora gives me that. She puts up with my slow stumbling plod with the patience of a canine saint. We walk at my pace because she knows I cannot walk at hers.

I have to be honest, at first my relationship with her was ambivalent. Did we really need a dog? And if we did, why a poodle? Why not something more masculine - a mastiff, bulldog or German shepherd? I asked myself that question again after being sarcastically wolf-whistled passing a building site. For weeks I used to walk her only after sunset. Wearing dark glasses. And a balaclava. I must have looked like Lord Lucan.

But now we have reached a gentle middle age together. She no longer sports that ridiculous bouffant and I have consigned the disguises to the dustbin. And although I don't walk her as much as I should, she is always there to help loosen stiff joints and encourage mobility. Flora is more than a pet.

To be perfectly honest I've never really 'got' pets. As a concept that is. I mean I can see the point in companion animals I suppose. Don't get me wrong - I've had my share of pets when I was young. Rodents, birds, tortoises – the usual suspects. And any number of fairground goldfish - one day wonders in every sense of the word.

And budgerigars. Incidentally what a large word for such a small bird. And such a strange word. But nowhere near so strange as the names I gave mine. I had two. One, a pale blue budgie, was called Kaiser Wilhelm. My albino was Hermann Goering.....

Yes.

OK this probably takes some explaining.

It was 1967 and there was a tune in the charts at the time called "I was Kaiser Bill's batman" by Whistling Jack Smith. He was, and I believe still is, the only souffleur ever to have a hit single and is a lasting testament to Andy Warhol's fifteen minutes of fame theory. There is even a video on Youtube if you want to share the experience of Jack in his pomp.... Bizarre but there you go - a Yorkshire budgie named after a Prussian emperor. Kaiser Bill.

Apart from that it was the usual assorted small rodents. Nothing desperately exciting. And a tortoise that lived at the bottom of the garden.

You're still thinking about Whistling Jack Smith aren't you? And hang on a minute - what about the Hermann Goering one? Don't let us forget that.

After all not many boys name budgerigars after war criminals. In fact I'm guessing that I was probably the only boy in Yorkshire who has ever named a budgie after the head of the Third Reich's Luftwaffe.

I can explain. No really - I can explain. Hard to imagine perhaps but Goering was not always the Nazi blimp of later years. In the First World War he was actually a dashing fighter pilot flying a snow white Fokker D7 on the western front. He even took over the Red Baron's squadron when Richtofen was shot down. Seriously. You can look this up.

So there you have it - snow white budgie, snow white biplane. Alles klar?

Names aside, some of my friends had much more interesting pets than my budgies. Billy Sharp, two streets away, kept a python called Ringo. Large predatory snakes were unknown in Yorkshire in the sixties and two streets was not far away enough for my mother's liking. "What if it escaped?" she would say "Charlie is only small". Charlie, my kid brother, may only have been two but, judging from the fight he put up at mealtimes, he would have been more than a match for the python.

Then there was Tommy Owen a gap-toothed fourth former with spectacles held together by plasters. Tommy was the boy who always appeared on both ends of the school photograph. He also held the school record for the longest period of detention - from 1963 to 1968 – his custody only curtailed by his inevitable expulsion. Tommy had a fruit bat called Noz, short for Nosferatu, that lived in a big enclosure in his garden and would eat pieces of satsuma from his hand. Noz had the dubious distinction of being the last pet ever brought into school for the 60s equivalent of Show and Tell. Madame Foiegras, the French teacher, was never quite the same again. And no, that isn't her real name.

Some pets just don't make any kind of sense. Like ferrets. As far as I'm concerned, any animal that uses razor sharp teeth as a means of conveying affection is wholly surplus to requirements. I can imagine Noah scratching his chin as he thumbs through the ark's passenger manifest like a nightclub bouncer "Sorry mate, you're not on the guest list. Can you swim?"

Pets have changed – gone are the mundane, replaced with tropical exotica. No kid wants a hamster when he can have an African land snail. And who wouldn't swap a goldfish for a stick insect or praying mantis. Our friends Eve and Drew were way ahead of the fashion with their vivarium full of tree frogs, like tiny emeralds and rubies on the branch, fed on a diet of live crickets. The crickets, enjoying unexpected freedom from their box, chirped away cheerily until the tree frogs gradually despatched them like U boats shadowing a convoy. From a survival standpoint, chirping is very bad. Sitting absolutely still and being very very quiet would be a much more prudent evolutionary tack. But the crickets never really quite got the hang of it. Until one November when several escaped and set up camp in the airing cupboard. For weeks afterwards Eve and Drew's house sounded like an English summer.

We are still not through the exotics phase. While my daughters have invariably had conventional pets - rabbits, guinea pigs and hamsters - Alex has always had a leaning towards the quirky. It is his thirteenth birthday this year and currently he has his heart set on a Jackson's chameleon. Not any old chameleon you understand - that would be much too dull. No, it has to be a Jackson's chameleon – if you have never seen one, and let's be honest you haven't, it looks like a triceratops on acid. Three huge facial horns and more colour changes than a Pink Floyd concert.

I think I'll stick with Flora. Talking of which it's time for a walk to shed some of those Christmas pounds. The drugs haven't really kicked in yet so I am unshaven and ever so slightly dishevelled. Still I cut quite a dash in my Russian hat, despite being a good half a stone heavier than November. I pick the lead off the hook. Flora bolts into the living room where I hear Alice taking softly to her.

"Doesn't Flora want a walk?" I ask.

"She does" calls Alice "But only if she can borrow your balaclava"

25th January 2010 ~ Be afraid. Be very afraid

Something happened this week that made me think about fear and the causes of fear. Something that made me confront old fears.

Think back to your childhood. What frightened you most? I'm guessing it wasn't global financial debts, Somali pirates or the melting of the polar ice caps. More likely it was something small. Spiders? Slugs? Mice perhaps? Everyone seems to have their own peculiar phobias. My own childhood nemesis was always moths. Not butterflies, only moths. Summer gardens alive with butterflies - Red Admirals, Painted Ladies or Marsh Fritillaries - fluttering from plant to plant were havens of enchantment. But the mere sight of an Emperor Moth, a Grey Dagger, or Brindled Beauty thudding into my bedside lampshade was enough to send me breathless and fearful into my parents' bed for comfort. Sleep made matters worse - I had nightmares about moths the size of table tennis bats getting inside my pyjamas and gnawing my tender parts. Or phalanxes of hawk moths crawling up my nose and eating my brain from within. Irrational I know but that's the thing with phobias. Besides moths are vegans.

Still, phobia trumps reason every time and my sleep was often broken by imagined visits from the Greater Ping Pong Wotsit Nibbler. Or Testiculosnapper Major, to give its Latin name.

As we go through life our fears change. Many childhood phobias vanish or lose their potency as we accrue the intellect and reasoning to recognise them for what they are. Take me - moths have no hold over me any more. I could comfortably cup a Lappet or a Foxglove Pug in my hand without flinching. But as irrational fears dwindle, others more tangible assume new significance. And suddenly I have a new reason to be afraid. We all do.

Because Catherine has passed her driving test. First time. With only five "minors"

OMG as Alice would say. Actually as she did say. The only person less than amazed was Catherine herself – "I expected to pass" she said with the kind of nonchalant confidence the Almighty reserves for teenagers.

£3.99 down the drain too – I had only picked up her L plates last week. I bought self-adhesive ones. "Good choice" the shop assistant said "The magnetic plates peel off over seventy". Unlike the cheapo adhesive variety I bought which seem to have been spot-welded in place.

Five minors is good. You are allowed fifteen before you fail. But a single "major" or "dangerous" fault means instant failure. So does any kind of examiner intervention. Apart from the usual whimpering. Or was that just my examiner?

The tea lady at work took eleven tests. And eighty four lessons at £20 a pop. She kissed the examiner on the lips when she finally passed. She was sixty four and most of the canteen staff thought they were signing a retirement card. Full marks for perseverance. Unlike Maggie, our new temp, who once held the Hampshire record for the shortest ever driving test – stopped after seven seconds, when she clipped the examiner's Mondeo while leaving the car park.

Maggie's test was already delayed while the examiner regained his composure after his previous ordeal. Smacking the dash to signal an emergency stop, he had somehow discharged the passenger airbag. He had red marks on his forehead where the blast had peppered him with his Murray Mints like a fusillade of grapeshot.

Of course, having a third driver in the household presents a number of logistical issues. Three into two doesn't go. Clearly she is not going to get behind the wheel of the Jag. Nor would she be seen dead driving Claire's Galaxy. So we find ourselves rummaging the free ads and wandering the forecourts along with flocks of other tyre-kickers to find a little runabout. Incidentally, what precisely do you learn about a car by kicking its tyres? Imagine if doctors used the same approach, only pronouncing you healthy as your cheek still tingled from the diagnostic slap across the face he had found it necessary to administer.

Picking a suitable car for a seventeen year old to drive is no trivial undertaking. Claire and I plan to use it too so there are a lot of plates to spin. It soon becomes obvious that Catherine's definition of 'suitable' shares little common ground with mine. I am thinking of slow cars with lots of metal, for protection. Catherine has a mental picture of snarly red Mazdas with tuned exhausts and sports steering wheels. I however am thinking along the lines of a Volvo with a lawnmower engine. If cars were dinosaurs, Catherine wants a velociraptor. I want a diplodocus. Claire just wants something girly. Before long, Catherine is sending subliminal 'roadster' messages to Claire. I sense an alliance forming.

Clearly this has to be stopped. Since I am paying, I award myself the casting vote. In fact the only vote. It is to be a second hand A Class Merc, I announce. With the lowest spec engine.

End of discussion.

And, to be honest, the Stuttgart Star is a pretty fair compromise. Like a four wheeled Tardis it will hold the whole family, including the dog. And the 1.4 is quick enough. "It's perky" I say to Catherine with my best winning smile. "more like Parky" mutters an unconvinced Catherine. The sunroof wins her over.

Catherine has christened the car Jasper. No, I don't know either.

This reminds me that my own driving licence is due up in a few months and I will need to look at renewing it. This is uncharted territory and I feel like a poker player turning over his cards. Aces? Busted flush? What will the DVLA deal me? Three years more motoring I hope. I'm certainly not ready to give up driving and they say you know in your own heart when it is that time.

I am just picking up the phone to call the DVLA when the doorbell rings. It is the man from the hospice collecting old woollens. I fetch three of my Aunt Kath's old Arrans. He shakes his head. "Hoffmannophila pseudospretella" he says. I look puzzled. "There" says David Attenborough, pointing to the evidence.

And he's right. Hoffmannophila pseudospretella. The Brown House Moth.

31st January 2010 ~ Nets

With piles of snow still on the ground outside the gym, it feels vaguely ridiculous to be donning cricket whites. Yet, along with several other dads, I have signed up for the winter nets. Even in our whites we look a motley crew, with young and old together. Yet here we are in January shivering in the nets, as the mighty leviathan that is the Bells Yew Green Fourth XI awakens from its winter slumber and stirs in readiness for the cricket season. Yes I know that's more than four months away, but believe me it's not a moment too soon. We need every minute of practice we can get. Even Alex has been roped in to bowl to the dads.

Time marches on and there's no escaping the fact that some of our team are not in the first flush of youth. Before you say anything, I number myself among them. Certainly few of us look much like our passport photos any more. The changing room smells less of wintergreen and Brut than of Horlicks and buttercup syrup. Kit bags are more likely to contain Saga magazine than Loaded or GQ. I wonder if I will be the first of the team to qualify for winter fuel payments. Fortunately the youngsters keep the average age of the team below three figures.

Back to the nets. In fairness, the 4th XI training needs are modest. The team could do with some help in the batting and bowling departments but apart from that we are in good nick. Oh and fielding I suppose. And a spare wicket-keeper wouldn't go amiss. Come to think of it, we're also missing a regular scorer. And supporters. Some days last season the groundsman even forgot to open the pavilion. It's enough to make us feel a bit unloved if we were the sensitive kind. Like the kid whose name everybody forgets.

But I'm a glass half full sort of person. I'm sure, come the first day of the season, that all our technical deficiencies will have been ironed out. We will take the field in May like a well oiled machine. In fact 'well oiled' was a description often applied to the 4ths last season. Mostly after the games. But we've been called worse. Alex asked me last season if the 4ths were atheists. "Why?" I said. He pointed to the opposition captain limbering up. "Because he says you haven't got a prayer". Cheeky monkey.

Any sports coach will tell you that exercise is the cornerstone of a serious training regime. There's no escaping the fact that my own training program has let me down. Over Christmas it has been less aerobics than chairobics. When the going gets tough, the tough reach for the Sky remote. The only six-packs to be seen here are in the fridge and that means getting up off the sofa. But I'm prepared to do the hard yards.

Diet is important too and we finely honed athletes have to be careful what we eat. "My body is a temple" I tell Claire one suppertime, declining the Matterhorn of steamed cabbage she is determined to place on my plate. "That fits" she snorts "you are about the size of the Acropolis". I turn to the kids "Your Mamma, she give me no respect" I mumble with a Brandoesque lisp.

The 4ths have generally embraced the nutritional part of training with - how shall I put it - more enthusiasm than technique. The bulging post-Christmas waistlines lend new meaning to the phrase 'middle order collapse'.

But food is only one component of diet. Fluid intake is vital for athletes and I've been learning about the value of sports energy drinks. They should be full of glucose and isotonic. And fluorescent orange. Despite this, vodka and Red Bull doesn't count apparently.

Of course I'm paying the price for this festive self-neglect in the nets. It takes longer to put on my pads than it did to put on the pounds. Reactions are slower, movements more ponderous and footwork non-existent. Imagine John Sargent with a bat in his hand and you're getting the picture. Our coach couldn't bring himself to watch last week and even the skipper is starting to look anxious. And it's only January.

On the other hand it's a morale booster for the youngsters doing the bowling. You can see the fast bowlers licking their lips like a pride of lions. They don't see a strokeplaying batsman in front of them so much as a stricken wildebeest bent on nothing more than survival. Already our numbers are dwindling. One of our new recruits is out for twelve weeks, after a bizarre DIY accident all but severed his thumb. I don't know - the lengths some people will go to rather than face the quicks!

And what a difference a year makes to the kids. This time last year Alex was full of enthusiasm and encouragement. It was all "Nice shot Dad" and "Great footwork". Not any longer. As adolescence tightens its malign grip, he is suddenly more openly critical. Still, Monday's nets were good. I was hitting the ball well. My cover drive was a recognisable imitation, and you would have identified my cut shot more often than not. I even managed a halfway decent impression of a pull. My mistake was to ask Alex for his opinion.

He looked me in the eye. "Let's face it Dad" he said "You bat like roadkill".

February

Boats, Baboons, Blues

7th February 2010 ~ Music

Sigmund Freud the psychiatrist was deeply suspicious of music. Of all the arts, it seemed to him the least amenable to his kind of scrutiny. So in August 1910, when he finally acceded to repeated requests to analyse Gustav Mahler, he did so with profound reticence. Indeed this was not psychoanalysis in the conventional sense, nor a meeting of equals. Although Freud was well-known in early twentieth century Vienna, Mahler occupied the status of demigod. Former director of the Vienna State Opera and principal conductor of the Vienna Philharmonic Orchestra, Mahler was also the composer of gigantic late Romantic symphonies.

Their encounter was at best a qualified success. Mahler entered the meeting as a giant of the Viennese cultural scene, but beset by marital problems. He left it strangely reinvigorated as Freud gave him a prolonged psychiatric handbagging. Although his meeting with Freud was something of an epiphany for Mahler, there is no evidence that Freud unearthed any great insights into Mahler's music. Mahler certainly, but not his music.

There is something about music that seems to speak to

parts of us that are outside the range of normal sensory input. When we look at a painting, our eyes detect colour, form, structure and narrative. In many respects, we can reduce the painting to these components, deconstructing the whole into separate packets to be subsequently reassembled by our cerebral cortex.

But music seems different. And the way we listen to music determines what we get from it. Tonality, form and narrative are all present but are somehow woven into a single seamless flow. Unless you're a musicologist, whose profession it is to reduce walls to bricks or windows to panes, music need not be dissected. It can simply be enjoyed. That's it - just enjoyed.

I've always had a soft spot for Desert Island discs, especially in the days of Roy Plomley. A bit of chat, a few quirky luxuries and some good tunes all based on the musical choices of hypothetical shipwreck survivors. It looks strange put like that. Mind you, the idea that one should be shipwrecked on a desert island for an eternity, yet still somehow have access to a decent hi-fi (and therefore presumably electricity) has never been adequately explained.

And another thing about shipwrecks - when the 'Abandon Ship' signal sounds over the Tannoy, I for one will not take this as a cue to rummage through my CD collection. Nor for that matter, will my first thoughts be to pick up the complete works of Shakespeare and a Bible. Nor any book. No I have a hunch that I will most likely devote my last moments on board to grabbing a life jacket.

Then I shall go and find a lifeboat. Ideally one that is not full of people carrying CDs and armfuls of books.

And what about the island? You're thinking tropical

palms and white sand, I'll bet. Not perhaps Cornwallis Island, a desert in the Canadian Arctic. A cold desert. A very, very cold desert. You can put the trunks away and start building a shelter. You will be rubbing penguins together for warmth. The latest Sugababes single will be no help at all when it comes to fending off polar bears or skinning seals.

Despite the engagingly potty idea behind the show, Desert Island Discs has stood the test of time, even outliving the odd presenter. But after 68 years on air, you'd expect the body count to be mounting up. And there must be hardly anyone left in the country to interview. But I'm ready. Along with my Oscar/Nobel/Booker prize acceptance speech, I have my music choices on a scrap of paper somewhere.

Oh go on then. Since you asked nicely...

They will probably be different tomorrow but here is what I might pick this week:

Tom Waits – 'Come on up to the house'. Despite lines like 'Come down off the cross, we can use the wood' this is a beautiful song about fear, comfort and acceptance all delivered in a voice that makes Louis Armstrong sound like a countertenor.

Richard Wagner – 'Parsifal' – conducted by Hans Knappertsbusch live from the Bayreuth Festival in 1951. I'd better explain this. Parsifal is about redemption and the Holy Grail. Put Dan Brown, Indiana Jones and Monty Python out of your mind for a minute, this is the real deal. The Bayreuth opera house, a popular haunt of Hitler was closed after the war by the Allies. The Festival reopened in 1951 with this performance as an act of purification. Nobody conducted Parsifal better than Knappertsbusch.

Nobody.

Keith Jarrett – 'The Koln concert'. A gift from my brother in law. Recorded in the mid 70s, this is some of the most ethereal jazz piano you will ever hear. Not funky (or jazzy). At the time of the concert, Keith was unwell and the piano was damaged and out of tune. Normally the queue at the box office for refunds would have been huge but Jarrett just sat down and improvised for two hours in a world of his own. Fetch a glass of wine, turn the lights down low and be bewitched.

Kate Rusby – 'Blooming Heather'. The Barnsley Nightingale sings this old Scottish folk ballad in a fragile child's voice that would melt any heart. I'm not biased. The fact she's from Yorkshire has nowt to do wi' it.

Jah Shaka – 'New Testament of Dub'. My brother first introduced me to the rumbling dub of Jah Shaka some twenty years ago. This is reggae for people without neighbours. Or who don't want neighbours. Shaka's sound system delivers his message over the kind of bass that loosens earwax. And probably brain cells.

Mariem Hassan – 'Alu Ummi'. I first heard this one night on Radio 3's Late Junction and was stunned. Taken from her album 'Shouka' this is a mesmeric tune from the Sahara delivered in Hassan's guttural Saharawi rasp. It takes a bit of getting used to. I think it's beautiful. Catherine said it sounds like an exorcism. Still, worth a punt on iTunes.

Uncle Earl – 'Streak of fat, streak of lean'. Old time fiddle-based mountain music but sung in Mandarin. Makes no sense whatsoever but I guarantee you won't be able to keep your feet still. Not that we Parkies can anyway.

Gillian Welch – 'Caleb Meyer'. Alcoholism, rape and homicide all in three minutes. Doesn't sound very uplifting but you couldn't be more wrong.

Gustav Mahler's 9th symphony with the Vienna Philharmonic Orchestra. And we're back where we began with the work Mahler had finished shortly before meeting Freud. And as much of the symphony was a reflection of Mahler's inner turbulence, so can the same be said of the performance. The recording I recommend was made at a concert on January 16, 1938 and conducted by Bruno Walter, a close personal friend of Mahler. The unrest and anxiety prevalent throughout Europe at that time seems to pervade the performance. There is an anguished yet valedictory quality to the playing. This is a historical document. Many of the performers on this recording knew that their days in Vienna were numbered. Some, like Walter himself, had firm plans to leave. And they were right – the ship was sinking.

Two months later the Wehrmacht marched into Austria and rounded up the orchestra's Jews. Suddenly music didn't matter any more.

13th February 2010 ~ Don't mention the PD

I make a point of running each blog past my wife and children before posting. Not because there's anything scurrilous or controversial but simply to give them an idea of what is forthcoming before it hits the World Wide Web. Catherine reads them. But for Alice and Alex, I think the blogs barely appear over the horizon. Alice would probably only read it if it appeared in Vogue or was endorsed by

Karl Lagerfeld. And for Alex, the blogs come a poor second to his DVD of great West Indian fast bowlers. Fair enough - given the choice between reading my meanderings or watching Curtly Ambrose scythe through the Australian top order, I know which I'd pick

Until recently, I didn't have the impression that Claire read them at all. But last week, over coffee, she said to me "You know something strange about your blogs?" I looked up. "You don't mention Parkinson's much" she said "In fact, some weeks you don't mention it at all".

Good point.

I don't think she meant it as a criticism. It was just an observation. But it got me thinking. And before long I have a whole bundle of questions in my mind. And I can't sleep. My mind is buzzing with these thoughts and it's three in the morning. Leaving aside the more pressing question of whether I try to sleep or just simply write this night off and press on till dawn, there are questions to answer.

If I don't write about PD, does it mean that it is not a major factor in my life?

Okay that's an easy one. PD is certainly a key part of my life. From fumbling with change, to spilling drinks, or tying my shoelaces, PD's unwelcome presence is always there.

Is it a form of denial? If I don't write about it, maybe it will go away?

No I don't buy this either. I don't delude myself that it's a mistaken diagnosis or that I don't need the medication. It isn't and I do. But that doesn't mean that I have to accept everything this condition throws at me. Acknowledging its existence is one thing but accepting its consequences is a very different kettle of fish.

Perhaps there is nothing new to say?

Possibly. Goodness knows, there are enough blogs and other websites on the Internet with practical advice on how to fight Parkinson's, how to secure those small victories in this endless war. Who needs my thoughts?

Maybe, like an embarrassing friend at a party, I just want Mr Parkinson to shut up. I know he won't leave, but if he can just stop reminding me of things, that would be a start. So in some subconscious way, perhaps I try not to encourage him. From the beginning, I have never wanted to ram Parkinson's down throats. The blog is on a Parkinson's website. You know I have Parkinson's. Enough said surely?

In any case, as my friend Tina from YAP says "I have Parkinson's, the Parkinson's does not have me". And that's a common rallying cry. You can be positive. My friend Bob the Biker would perhaps go further and say you must be positive. Bob has a Honda Goldwing so he knows a thing or two about motorbikes. From his approach to his PD journey, I'd say he knows a thing or two about Parkinson's as well. Besides, on a Goldwing, you'd want to share that journey!

My feeling is this. I mention the Parkinson's when, and only when, it impinges directly on my subject matter. So if I'm writing about music for instance, the PD is nowhere to be seen - it's probably skulking in a corner. On the other hand, if I'm writing about cricket, hang gliding, pole vaulting, or bobsleigh, there is a fair bet that the PD will have some bearing on the outcome. So I'll write about it.

Sure, things happen more slowly. If I'm in the supermarket queue ahead of you, you might want to look for a different checkout. By the time I have finally bagged up my groceries you could have learned a foreign language. You could be paying for your mandarins in Mandarin. There's no such thing as Fast Track with me. It's the same in the post office. By the time I have paid for six first-class stamps and a postal order, the man at the adjacent counter has changed nationality.

Another thing about Parkinson's is the influence it has on others. Believe me when I say that I now have the power to determine which clothes my friends wear. Really. If you are going out to dinner with friends, you would normally dress up, right? Best bib and tucker? Not at the Stamfords'. And especially if you're seated next to me. When I'm snorkelling my way through a bowl of minestrone, you don't want to be anywhere near the epicentre. Especially in that new white Thai silk sarong. Everyone wears jeans and old clothes. Don't say I didn't warn you.

But let's make no bones about it. Like the words to the Catholic Mass, Parkinson's is "in my thoughts, on my lips and in my heart" every day. But that's my problem not yours. Besides, we don't stop living just because we have Parkinson's. Life goes on. There is money to be earned, bills to pay, friends to enjoy, plans to make, family to love.

So if it's all the same to you, I'd like to keep it in perspective. My perspective.

So don't mention the Parkinson's. I mentioned it once but I think I got away with it

20th February 2010 ~ Holidays again

The end of February is fast upon us and, as usual, we

have put off organising a family holiday until it's nearly too late. Choosing the destination is a logistic conundrum similar to organising the Normandy landings. Indeed merely securing a brief time window in my children's busy Facebook, X-box, PS3, or Wii calendars is a challenge akin to buying Centre Court tickets for Wimbledon. "I can give you half an hour on Thursday" says Alice dismissing me with all the tenderness of Sir Alan Sugar.

Reconciling the multifaceted and extraordinarily detailed holiday needs of my teenage divas and their younger brother, to say nothing of Claire and I, makes the Good Friday agreement look like a bus ticket. So where do you find a holiday that has designer retail outlets, ready access to international cricket, an opera house, and several hundred Facebook friends? Oh and a beach.

Apart from the Caribbean that is – we're not made of money.

Invariably our thoughts turn to past holidays.

Like the narrowboat.

A week spent pub-hopping our way up and down the Grand Union Canal in August sounded idyllic. And for the other four members of the family, it probably was. But then they were not standing for hours, rain-lashed, at the tiller, in the most unseasonal August weather since records began. Nor were they in a constant wrestling match to maintain control of what amounts to a 12 ton aquatic shopping trolley with a wonky wheel. Not surprisingly, a narrowboat charts a course that is governed only partly by the tiller as anyone who has seen a 66 footer sawtoothing its way along in a cross wind can testify.

The Parkinson's lends a certain additional frisson of

excitement to the simplest of manoeuvres. According to the book, mooring a narrowboat is no more complex than parallel parking. In theory. In the hands of a Parky novice however, anything is possible. After one overconfident effort ended with more smashed crockery than a Greek wedding, I became aware that the handful of disinterested onlookers had swollen to the kind of crowd more commonly associated with a premiership football fixture. "Are you mooring it or scuttling it?" shouted one wag. We didn't stay long.

Of course, none of these navigational vagaries would matter one jot were it not for the fact that British canals in August are as busy as the M25 in rush hour. It's bumper-to-bumper. OK, tailgating at 4 knots is probably not a true white knuckle moment. And your life doesn't exactly flash before you when overtaken at a searing 6 knots on a blind bend. But then nor is it the picture of pastoral meandering so vividly portrayed in the brochure. For that matter, being pelted with traffic cones in a cutting near Banbury wasn't in the flyer either.

So canals are out the reckoning. We have ruled out safari parks too. I have decided that the natural habitat for viewing wild animals is television. Not cars.

As they drive around safari parks like Woburn or Longleat, the thoughts of most visitors are focused on the lion enclosure and the possibility, however remote, that these highly evolved yet reclusive carnivores might suddenly take a disproportionate interest in their vehicle or its occupants.

In concentrating on the big cats, they have rather taken their eye off the ball. Because the real danger lies elsewhere. I remember visiting Longleat around 1970 with my family. We were travelling in my father's latest pride and joy, a spanking new Audi 100. Littering the monkey enclosure, like some post-apocalyptic urban art installation, was an unsettling amount of chrome debris. The monkeys looked up as we drove in and the colour drained from my father's face. "Don't make eye contact" said father, as a congress of baboons circled the car. The first to jump on the roof elicited a brisk wartime "keep calm" from my mother and something like a whimper from my father, soon becoming an open-mouthed wail as the driver side windscreen wiper was torn off.

The baboons had barely started. Over the next few minutes they showed us just how many parts of a car are detachable. With a little simian initiative, that is.

Father closed his eyes in despair as the baboons visited an orgy of destruction upon car and van alike. It was like the road to Basra. Anything that could be removed from a car was. We had moved barely fifty yards before my father realised we no longer had wing mirrors. A creche of baboon babies were using them as castanets. Mother turned round and gave us a "whatever you do, don't laugh" look as the hubcaps were tossed like Frisbees from monkey to monkey. Best of all was the dominant male conducting an imaginary orchestra with the remains of the aerial, whilst simultaneously urinating over the windscreen. You never got that from Solti or Karajan. "He's doing a wee wee" offered the six-year-old Charlie helpfully. I remember the taste of blood in my mouth as I bit my tongue to stifle a giggle. As the baboons moved on, my father breathed a premature sigh of relief. There was a loud crack." Oh my God - what was that?" he shouted. Nobody said anything - it looked like part of the roof rack.

That was forty years ago. We never went back.

And after an evening's discussion, we are still no closer to finding a holiday. Everything has been suggested from a week in Blackpool to a cruise on the Queen Mary. You name it, we've discussed it – trains, planes and automobiles. Hotels, boats, castles and Winnebagos.

Of course it's not helped by my escalating aversion to air travel. Even before the PD, I would quiver to the point where stewardesses would enquire after my health. " Afraid of flying?" they would ask. "No, afraid of crashing" I would reply.

And the whole routine with the shoes is calculated to cause maximum Parky embarrassment. I have always had feet that were - how shall I put this - a little less fragrant than Mary Archer. Claire says there would be no need to pack my shoes with explosives. The mere act of removing my cricket trainers would be sufficient to bring down most airliners.

My cousin's partner is an airline pilot. Pick your worst airline stories. Air rage, drunken passengers, births and deaths - he's seen it all. But nothing tops the occasion a passenger collapsed in the aisle. As a stewardess loosened his clothing and began to pummel his chest to revive him, the inevitable call went out over the Tannoy "Is there a doctor on board?" At the back of the aircraft, a man got up and walked towards the patient. He knelt down, tapped the stewardess on the shoulder and said

"Excuse me, but I ordered a hot panini ten minutes ago"

26th February 2010 ~ Footy

I've been learning a new language. Actually it's less a language than a group of phrases that I can use to mask my blatant ineptitude. Sometimes that's all you need. I have this theory that, whenever you go abroad for instance, you really only really need to know the local words for 'please', 'thank you' and 'the taxi fare cannot possibly be that much'. If you're feeling adventurous you could always try 'I only want to hire the taxi not buy it'. Probably best not to press the point though. Sarcasm rarely translates into other languages.

Actually I've forgotten the most important one - beer. In fact ordering a beer in a bar is all that remains of my dismal attempts to learn Italian in the 1980s. And it's not as though I hadn't applied myself to the task, sitting up in bed late at night with my matching Berlitz book and CD repeating phrase after phrase. "Our tour guide has been struck by lightning", "The cockroaches are watching television" and "If you tilt your head, the bleeding will stop". Scary place Italy.

I perked up when I reached the phrase book's food and drink section. With due diligence, I could order seafood in Naples, game in Tuscany, and olive oil in Puglia. I went further than just ordering a bottled beer, as the course suggested. I could even order draught beer. I can tell you're impressed. "Una birra a la spina, per favore" I said loudly one evening in a bar in Rome, parading my hard-won knowledge. "Scusi?" said the waiter, leaving me pointing red-faced to the beer tap. Snort of laughter from wife. Giggles from kids. And I was doing so well.

But this is nothing compared with the linguistic challenge I face every Sunday morning, when Alex plays Under 13 football for his local club. I should probably fess up - I know absolutely squat about football. Well, I know the rules and can explain the offside law but then that's carried on the Y chromosome anyway. It's innate in the same way that geese fly south for winter or bees find nectar. You just know it.

No, it's the terminology I mean - it's a foreign language to me. I wouldn't know a wingback from a wing-nut or a spread midfield from a flat back four. When someone shouts "pick your man up!", my first reaction is that it's not allowed. But then I used to watch Leeds in the 70s and the rules at Elland Road seemed somehow more elastic than at other grounds.

The lingo of football is strangely abstract. "Don't let him turn you" I heard one of the opposition's dads yell at his son. Turn you? Into a frog? To the Dark Side perhaps? Now I think about it, the boy's name was Luke. Chubby lad though - more Pie Stalker than Skywalker.

But I'm a fast learner and over the last couple of months I've learnt lots. For instance "No-nonsense player" is footballspeak for "gormless psychopath" while "goal sniffer" can either mean a striker with the happy knack of being in the right place at the right time or, just as easily, mean a player who takes root somewhere in the 6 yard box, too lazy to run around the field chasing the ball. There are tactical terms too. "Tuck in!" means "Defend". Unless you are Luke of course to whom it means "Scan the horizon for bacon sarnies". "Go wide!", shouted at wingers, means "Run as close as you can to the touchline". A pointless order for Luke who is already as wide as he can be without his mum buying shorts the next size up.

I've been puzzling on the subject of football nicknames too. There seem to be certain rules. If your surname is only one syllable long, your nickname will automatically involve the addition of the letter Y. Bloggs becomes Bloggsy, Smith becomes Smithy, Banks becomes Banksy, Scott becomes Scotty and so forth. This doesn't apply to polysyllabic surnames. Venegoor of Hessellink-Y somehow doesn't sound very chummy. You don't often hear "Oi, Venegoor of Hessellink-Y, over here son, on my head!"

Some clubs seem to have Ronseal nicknames - they do exactly what they say on the tin. A few weeks ago, the team were kicked off the park by the opposition midfielders. But let's face it, Nosher, Gnasher and ASBO were as uncompromising a midfield trio as their names implied, and tackled players with impunity, in a manner that would not have been out of place at Twickenham. When eventually penalised they were keen to inform the referee that he was a Cyclops of ambiguous genealogy (go on, you're nearly there).

Our team played bravely for a while, but lost heart a bit when the sixth goal went in. After the ninth, they fell apart. But this is a new young team, a bit like Busby's Babes, and they are improving every day. Still, as learning curves go, they don't get much steeper than this. Games played: 10, games won: 1, goals scored: 4, goals conceded: 58, current league position: bottom.

I like to think that I'm optimistic but the team coach, Tim, is in a different league. Premiership optimism. And it rubs off. Despite being on the receiving end of biblical annihilations each week, the team is still together. After each Sunday's crushing defeat, Tim somehow picks his young charges up at Tuesday training, dusts them down, and prepares them for next Sunday.

Training seems to be about shapes. When they're not weaving between cones, the lads are forming triangles. The coaches talk a lot about triangles in training. Three players passing the ball between them, that sort of thing. Alex's team do a lot of three player triangles in the matches - unfortunately, two of the three players are usually wearing opposition shirts.

The team's new kit is long overdue. Sponsored by an Arab sheik (I'm not making this up), it should make all the difference. So far this season, the team has played most games dressed like Confederate foragers. No two look alike. When the kit arrives, they will look like Juventus. Probably won't play like Juventus but at least they will look the part.

At training, the kids wear tracksuit tops with their initials over the chest. Thus Alex Stamford becomes AS, and so on. Which is fine in most cases. But other nearby clubs have had problems. Ben Oliver could never understand why people near him held their noses and laughed. And Owen O'Halloran was routinely greeted at training sessions with a chorus of Frankie Howerd titters. Kids can be cruel.

Andy Stevens-Stock's tracksuit was lost in the post. It's probably for the best.

So there I was, last weekend, shivering and quivering on the sidelines along with the other dads, trying to sound knowledgeable, while the team battled hard to keep the scoreline halfway respectable. A 3-0 defeat on our own park. Were the boys dejected? Hardly. In the context of this season, that almost qualified for a lap of honour.

The opposition coach summed up the game by speaking in tongues "He was sick as a parrot to go for an early bath during the transfer window but at the end of the day, it's a funny old game of two halves and, all credit to the lads, who are over the moon, we keep reminding ourselves to take each game as it comes because you have to play ninety minutes of football and each game is a six pointer but it's another clean sheet in our cup run"

I have no idea what it meant. It's all Greek to me.

March

Stars and Supermarkets

6th March 2010 ~ Supermarket Sweep

In pretty much every episode of the Lone Ranger, there was a point, usually just after the William Tell overture, where the baddies got away, and the trail went cold. And so did the show. Then mysteriously, after a day or two of uncomfortably introspective faffing about in the desert, the dynamic duo would stumble across hoof prints. Tonto would put his head to the ground and listen.

"Three horses - maybe two days ago - and lame donkey - heavy prints - many guns - lead north" he said.

"By Jiminy - they're headed to Devil's Creek" said the Lone Ranger "We'll cut them off at Cactus Gulch"

"More" said Tonto "man on lead horse called Frank Cartwright. Him lose much money today to Indian scout"

The Lone Ranger is gobsmacked "How can you know that Tonto?"

Tonto held up the evidence "Him drop credit card. Shopping, Kemo Sabe?"

Okay I made up the last bit. But as a kid, Tonto's deductive skills impressed me no end. How could he be so sure that they were on the trail of Mexican bandits? How did he get it right all the time? Or were there dozens of episodes we were never allowed to see where Tonto completely screwed up. And the Lone Ranger ambushed a Women's Institute picnic instead of the high Sierra hideout of the notorious Hole in the Carpet Gang. Tonto would put his head in his hands. "Tonto get coat, Kemo Sabe".

I think I would have made a good Indian scout. I've been applying these same skills while shopping in the local supermarket. Before you say anything, I don't get dressed up as a Potawatomi brave to do my shopping. Well, not every week. Nor do I lie in the car park smelling tyre tracks "1998 BMW 3 series, two kids and a Rottweiler called Fang. Stuck in M25 contraflow. Near Cactus Gulch".

No, forget the car park, I'm talking about the contents of shopping baskets. I'm not a nosy person but I can't help looking at other people's shopping whilst affecting an air of nonchalance. If I'm waiting in the queue at the supermarket, there's precious little else to do - it's what computer people call 'downtime'. With PD, I am aware that, in the future, I will be spoilt for downtime, so I try to use each moment of 'uptime' to some useful purpose. Besides, the contents of the trolley or basket read like haikus - slices of people's lives. Who needs ink blots when you can extract a detailed psychological profile from what people put in their shopping baskets.

I'll give you an example: small white loaf, a pack of rich tea biscuits and two tins of deluxe cat food. Is the owner (a) Ottavio, a 28-year old Italian graphic designer who has just launched his own dotcom that afternoon, or (b) a 79-year old widow called Mabel whose best friend Smudge is 'such a fussy eater'?

OK, that was an easy one. You all got Ottavio, right?

Want to try another – Four pack of Carling, Babycham, family size bag of Doritos, pack of condoms and a tube of Clearasil? What can we say of him?

Is he (a) Charles, a suave, urbane stockbroker with a yacht moored in the bay or (b) Carl, a spotty teenage optimist whose evening is definitely not going to pan out the way he thinks. Pound to a penny his teddy bear will be the only thing he snuggles up to tonight.

There you go – you're getting the hang of this. Before you know it, you've turned into Cracker or Hercule Poirot without the daft 'tache. At least it helps while away the hours spent either shopping or queueing to pay. And you'd be amazed how many hours that can be.

Calculators ready?

I am fifty three. I am a big boy now and have been doing my own shopping for the last thirty five years. Despite this, Claire despatches me to Tesco with a lengthy list containing instruction more detailed than the tempo markings on a Mahler symphony. Often she will talk me through it in advance 'Passion fruit fat-free low sugar yogurt from managed Brazilian rainforest – they're on the shelf beside the cholesterol-lowing ones but with a different colour lid. Only buy if the two-for-one offer is still on. Otherwise buy the mango and guava fruit corners on the next shelf under the kiwi and banana milkshakes." Being a man I hear the word "yogurt". And nothing else. I make a mental note – 'buy some yogurt'.

When the shopping list runs to two pages of micrographic writing, I know I'm in trouble and try to recruit help. Alice never comes – I am far too unfashionable to be seen with her. And Alex would rather do homework. Shopping with dad is that enticing. If Catherine comes with me, we speed-shop. And we improvise. Claire always interrogates us on return with the same question "Did you get every item on the list?" and I've learnt that cheery responses like "Quite a few of them" and "Well over half" do not afford Claire the level of reassurance she is seeking. But the shopping list is a cry for help really.

But I digress – back to the shopping. On average the weekly shop takes say sixty minutes. Actually it's probably longer now I think about it but we'll stick with sixty. Of that sixty minutes, perhaps ten are spent in the queue at the tills. Thus far I have spent some three hundred-odd hours standing in a queue to pay. That's three hundred hours of downtime. The equivalent of ten test matches. Five premiership football seasons. The combined flight time of the entire Apollo moon landing program. Some insect species evolve in less time than I have spent queueing. If you add the hours of wandering like a zombie up and down the aisles, it amounts to more time than I spent in lectures as an undergrad. And I did a four-year course.

All in all, I have spent - get this - the waking hours of three entire months of my life in a supermarket. And nearly two weeks alone standing at the till pretending to be Tonto. I bet Tonto never struggled to open the carrier bags. He would have gestured to Tiffany on the till "Squaw's work". Nor, I imagine, would he shakily spill his change on the ground, and watch in misery as nearby children helped themselves to the larger denomination coins. Apparently the supermarket is an extension of the playground and the rules of "Finders keepers" still hold sway here. It's not every day you spend £9.33 on a Crunchie. I shall watch out for the Locust children next time.

I suppose I shouldn't complain. The other day I read that an ordinary loaf of bread cost nearly a million pounds in Zimbabwe. I phoned Charlie.

"Amazing" he said "I didn't know they had Waitrose over there".

13th March 2010 ~ Facebook

Facebook brings out the worst in me. My family know that if there is one subject that lights the blue touch paper with me, it's Facebook. I'll tell you now, this is going to be a rant. So, if you don't want to know the score, look away now.

But what, I hear you asking, is it about Facebook that so thoroughly gets your goat? What piques you? As much as anything else, I resent the mangling of the English language. Let me give you one example -- "friend". A noun you might understandably be forgiven for thinking. It is after all a word derived from old English, Norse and Old High German, and has served the English language well as a noun for perhaps a thousand years, give or take a few centuries. But no longer. "Friend" has been press-ganged into action as a verb. And all the fingers point accusingly at Facebook. Apparently you 'friend' someone. You don't befriend them. You don't invite them to be your friend -- and incidentally is there any more ridiculous concept than inviting someone to be your friend? They either are or are not. No, you friend them. Grrrr.

Even the term "social networking" irritates me. It's the kind of asinine circumlocution used by management types. You know, the ones who would refer to death as a "negative care outcome" if they were doctors. The same people who talk about 'rightsizing' a company's workforce, as though the neutrality and positivity of the word 'right' will somehow blind employees to the empty offices of friends and their own groaning In trays. These are weasel words and 'social networking' is similar nonsense. I don't have a social network -- I have friends. I talk eagerly to my friends, I do not network with them.

And another thing - the little thumbs up sign under each posting. So under a posting of say "Jon Stamford has been to visit his neurologist today", people can click a box to indicate say "Tristan McFlurry likes this". What? Likes what? Likes the fact that I see my neurologist? Perhaps there should also be a button, for Roman emperors and the like, to give a thumbs down. But why have a box at all. All we really expected to vote on each other's posts?

And I think this must be an age thing. Perhaps I just don't get it. I joined Facebook to keep in touch with friends that I haven't seen for a while. Isn't that what it's about?

Every one of my friends on Facebook is there for a reason -- because I care about them and am interested in knowing what they're doing. It brings me closer to people I haven't seen in a while. It shortens the distance. I laughed aloud that Isla's two-year-old son Gareth was brushing his teeth in the dog's water bowl. I want to know about my Maltese exile friend Jack's big innings. And Juliet's tales of the dog-rabbit. I love to hear from the other side of the world about Dizzy Izzy and her stories, about Lucia on the trapeze, Kent's latest recipe, and Jolie's sailing. I want to hear what Angel did in Harrods. I loved the pictures of Plum dressed as a gangster's moll at a wedding and of Francesca's dogs at the show. These are real friends and real events. I may be many miles from them, and have not seen them for ages, but by being my friends on Facebook, I can be with them. And they can be with me. My Facebook friends are just that. Friends. Plain and simple.

But even the briefest of conversations with Catherine and Alice, and being teenagers that's as much as I ever hope for, shows me to be in a minority of one. Both of the girls have the kind of social networks on Facebook that would fill a moderate sized football stadium. If the people were real that is. And I think that's my point. My friends are real flesh and blood friends. I exchange information with them as they would if they were sat opposite me in the snug of the Toad and Turnip. With teenagers it seems to be a race to see who can collect the most friends on Facebook. I suppose it is no more demented than cigarette cards or bubblegum wrappers were in the 1960s. Or Pokémon for instance.

But what disturbs me most is the blurring between fantasy and reality. I am bombarded by "news items" about farming. You might be forgiven for thinking that many of my friends have turned their backs on the city and are retiring to a simpler Mediaeval agrarian lifestyle. Perhaps they're shunning the excesses of urban life in the 21st century? Perhaps like the St George's Hill Diggers, they are making a political statement about the ownership of land? Noble and elevated motives all.

If any of this were real, that is. For this is an imaginary farm, stocked with imaginary animals in imaginary buildings and fields. Imaginary events taking place in this imaginary world.

That's all well and good, as long as it all stays in the imagination.

For the last three years, I've been part of a clinical trial about non-motor symptoms in Parkinson's disease. They ask me a lot of questions, and test my memory and reflexes and so forth. One of the questions they ask is along the lines of "do you ever have difficulty distinguishing reality and fantasy?" Perhaps I should say "yes I have imagined a farm, and it's real and my friends help me and I share crops with them." I can just imagine their reaction "It's okay Jon, just slip your arms into this funny white jacket and don't worry about the absence of armholes". Off to the real Funny Farm.

Okay so let's lay down some ground rules. Firstly I am not interested in Farmville. I do not care that people have built imaginary barns, piggeries, chicken coops and so forth. Nor do I want to share imaginary gifts. Nor be paid imaginary bundles of dollars or bags of gold. If you want to send the real stuff, drop me an e-mail and I'll give you a PO box number. But imaginary stuff, I can take it or leave it. My imagination plays enough tricks on me without pandering to its worst excesses.

Nor do I wish to complete questionnaires entitled "Which type of amoeba would you be?" or what type of fizzy drink would you be -- champagne since you ask -- or which astronaut were you in a former life? Life is too short for this stuff.

Nor will I become a friend of 'laughing at the sad bits in films' or 'knowing Pi to five hundred decimal places'. And as for all those bizarre groups that people join, I give up.

What kind of person would join a group entitled "I will go slightly out of my way to step on that crunchy looking leaf". There is even one entitled "I Secretly Want To Punch Slow Walking People In The Back Of The Head". Not many Parkies there I would hazard a guess.

Still thinking of poking me? Think twice.

21st March 2010 ~ Seeing Stars

Like the light bulb that would appear above a character's head to signify some moment of passing brilliance, I always assumed that seeing stars was a sort of cartoon shorthand and nothing more. That was until a few weeks ago when I discovered the hard way that the sliding glass door to the conservatory was closed rather than open.

You do indeed see stars. For me the indignity was compounded by bending my spectacles and leaving a clearly discernible face print on the glass, rather like the Turin Shroud. Predictably sympathy with my dazed plight was rather outweighed by laughter from the family. The same happens in cricket when a player is -- how shall I put this -- torpedoed amidships. While a blow on the arm or to the ribs has the physio running onto the pitch with a kit bag full of mystery salves and sprays, the same injury to the batsman's more delicate parts raises a sardonic cheer from spectators and the full gamut of titters and guffaws from the opposition players. I remember one player last year felled in such a fashion. For a minute, he thought he was going to die. Then for several minutes more, he hoped he was going to die.

I was reminded of this as I sat for a moment or two on the floor fiddling with my spectacles whilst I waited for the constellation of stars to return to their rightful places in the heavens. I quite forgot why I was going to the conservatory anyway. By the time the stars had cleared, so had my memory, wiped clean like one of those dodgy cassettes of lesser-known Motown hits that Fat Phil at the Hare and Hounds sold from the boot of a rusty Sierra.

I was looking for my telescope.

Yes you read that right. There's no escaping the fact, and I should probably come clean, but I am ... an astronomer.

There, that's a weight off my mind. I have lived with this dark secret for nearly 40 years. And throughout most of those, even my friends never guessed. Sure there would be tell-tale signs. The star chart in the loft, eyepieces sometimes left unnoticed on the piano. Occasional furtive glances upwards on a clear night. But for the most part, I have kept this hidden.

Cut to television documentary

Interviewer in full view of camera. A man we know only as 'Mr S' is silhouetted against a backdrop. His voice has been changed.

Interviewer (*to camera*): Tonight on Hard Walk, we are going to look at a hidden craze of middle-aged men and the effect it has on their lives. My first guest is a man who does not wish to be identified but we will call him Mr S.

Interviewer (*sympathetically*): Mr S, when did you first think you might be an astronomer?

Mr S (trembling voice): I was at school. It all started quite innocently. Some of my mates had a pair of binoculars. They were looking at the moon with them. Of course I was shocked. But then one of them asked me if I wanted to take a look at the moon. Of course I said no. But they kept going on about it. So I thought "what's the harm"? So I just took a quick look at one of the features on the moon – Mare Tranquillitatis I think..

.

(*Pause*)

Interviewer: But surely you could have walked away. You could just have said no, couldn't you?

Mr S: Of course you think you can control it, maybe a couple of minutes looking at craters of the moon, half an hour watching meteors, maybe a nebula or two. But before you know it, it's controlling you. And suddenly you find you're doing the hard stuff -- galaxies, globular clusters, outer planets, Saturn's rings.

Interviewer: But it wasn't just the stars was it?

Mr S: No. It was much worse. I was buying ... books. Star charts. That sort of thing.

Interviewer: When did your family begin to suspect you were an astronomer?

Mr S: I think it was the woolly hat. I bought a woolly hat and gloves so I could stay out longer to observe the stars. I even had a notebook to record my observations. Then one day, my brother found my Thermos. I knew the game was up.

Interviewer: How did your family react?

Mr S: They were brilliant. I don't know what I expected but they were really supportive. It must have been really tough for them, having a son who was an astronomer.

Interviewer: And I believe your mother helped?

Mr S: Yes she bought a T-shirt. On the front it said "Astronomer" and underneath that it said "and proud". But by then I was quite open about it. I would even read astronomy books in public. I didn't force it down people's throats but I was comfortable with it.

Interviewer: Do you think living conditions contribute to the rise in astronomy among youngsters?

Mr S: Yes, very much so. Some kids are lucky -- they might live in the city, where the bright streetlamps prevent them from getting their fix. Slowly but surely, they can be weaned off the stars. But I had no such luck. My school had an observatory, sited on a hillside and free from the streetlamps of the town. Worse still, they had a gigantic 18th-century telescope, at the time the most powerful in any school in Britain.

Interviewer: Was it a struggle?

Mr S: One thing led to another. By the time I left school, I had gone as far as you can -- comets, asteroids, planetary nebulae, constellations, conjunctions and sunspots. I've even done eclipses.

But you need to understand that it's not just an addiction. For many astronomers, it's a lifestyle choice. But we still face terrible prejudice from the general public.

Interviewer: Thank you Mr S.

(*Turns to camera*)

If you've been affected by any of the issues raised in this program, the helpline number will appear on screen in a minute.

(*Music swells, studio darkens*)

Announcer: And here is that number again.

(*number flashes on screen*)

Astronomers Anonymous. Ask for Jon.

28th March 2010 ~ Aaron the angry aardvark

The laws of probability dictate that an infinite number of chimpanzees sat at an infinite number of typewriters would eventually type the entire works of Shakespeare. The same laws of probability mean that they're going to write a whole lot of gibberish as well. But everything has a price. For every Shakespeare sonnet that emerges from Bonzo's typewriter, we will probably have to endure any number of simian limericks. But eventually the chimps will get there. King Lear? A walk in the park. The Tempest? A breeze.

I work for a living as a writer. Words are my bread and butter. And the ways in which I put those words together means a lot to me. It's not like turning on a tap or milking a cow. Some days I feel like Shakespeare, some days like Bonzo. Some days the words flow onto the page, perfect and fully formed. Beautiful lyrical passages waltzing from mind to paragraph in clear choreography.

Other days I'm Bonzo, staring uncertainly at the keyboard, wondering whether to bite my nails or pick my nose. Unsure what comes next. This word, that word, right word, wrong word, wrong place, right place, resting. Staccato statements. Terse tangles. Or even that worst kind of inertia, writer's block.

There is nothing a writer fears more than writer's block -- that point where all your creativity has been dispatched to the Russian front and you find yourself sitting at a typewriter or word processor, without the slightest idea of how to begin, or even what to begin. You write a few words, cross them out, then write more, repeating this cycle with increasing desperation. Some days it just won't come. But writers block is more than just a mere inconvenience -- it can become all-consuming, like Jack Nicholson, endlessly typing "all work and no play makes Jack a dull boy" in The Shining.

If writer's block is a problem, the fear of it is almost worse. And that fear of writer's block can drive men to their deaths. Ernest Hemingway, who wrote more and better than most, bagging Pulitzer and Nobel prizes on his way, was beset with fear that his writing had lost its potency. But let's be honest, after you win the Nobel Prize for literature, the bar is set pretty high. Eventually, as his own sternest critic and unable to find a solution on the typewriter, he found a very different and altogether more decisive solution with a shotgun.

Some call it Blank Page Syndrome. Faced with a blank piece of paper and a typewriter (or nowadays an empty computer screen) how do you start? Every piece of writing, scientific or poetic, narrative or descriptive, starts with a single word. Simple really, yet writers agonise more over that first word then over the hundreds which follow. It's all about getting started. And the more I think about it, the more I sense the parallels with Parkinson's and its inability to transfer thought to act -- to start walking. We know how to walk, what to do, how we put one foot in front of another. We just can't do it that's all. So we stand, counting to ten, or dancing to rhythms in our head, anything that helps us trick our bodies into unwanted movement. It's Walker's Block. Once we're going, we're fine.

Walker's Block or Writers Block - it's the same thing. We writers play tricks with ourselves, looking for some stimulus, some trigger to the imagination. Some writers pick words randomly from the dictionary, and construct a contrived narrative. Others pick letters and look for words starting with those letters: Apple, aardvark, angry, ankle, and that sort of thing.

So one day, Aaron the angry aardvark was ambling along when he twisted his ankle on an apple.

It's not Shakespeare is it? And to be honest it's not really me -- even if "Aaron The Angry Aardvark" sounds like a series of children's books.

And the Internet is a veritable cornucopia of advice on how to overcome writer's block. Watch a movie -- read a book -- have a bath -- mow the lawn. One 'solution' ran along the lines of "write a word. Then write another word. Then make a sentence. Then add another sentence. Make a paragraph. Then make another paragraph. Then before you know it you've got something." Gosh -- you don't say. That's right out of the 'pull yourself together' school of psychiatry.

Writing is deeply personal, and we each try to find our own solutions to writer's block. My own approach is to pour myself a beer, put on a Frank Zappa album at window rattling volume and play some enthusiastic air guitar. Surprisingly effective -- except on days that I'm in the office.

In any case if that doesn't work, there's always Aaron The Angry Aardvark.

Ultimately it's all just words and letters whether we are Shakespeare or Bonzo. The playwright Harold Pinter was once at a reception when a woman introduced him to her five-year-old son. "This is Mr Harold Pinter". The boy looked understandably blank. "Mr Pinter is a very good writer." The little boy looked Pinter up and down and turned to his mother.

"But can he do a W?"

April

Trains and Teeth

4th April 2010 ~ Gardening

I've never been a keen gardener. I've always felt that is best left to others. Mostly this attitude stems from my childhood because, when I was young, we had a gardener. That makes it sound much more grand than it really was -- visions of huge baronial estates, with peacocks strutting under cedar trees. The sound of croquet mallets echoing across manicured lawns perhaps.

Nothing could be further from the truth. We had a small patch of lawn, the usual shrubs and small trees, and flower beds around the patio. And we had Mr Potterton.

Mr Potterton had showed up one day on his bicycle, doffing his cap and asking my mother whether she needed the services of a gardener. Mr Potterton reminded me vaguely of a cross between Cpl Jones in Dads Army and the major in Fawlty Towers. He was an old man, rather short, very earnest and keen to work. Since his retirement, he had lived alone -- his wife had died some years earlier -- and his daughter fretted that he was not getting out and about much. So she encouraged him to get on his bike and find a job. We were the first door he knocked upon.

My mother, soft as ever, offered him a job. So the following Tuesday, Mr Potterton knocked on our door again and asked what work he was to do that day. My mother suggested that perhaps he could do some pruning. He seemed delighted. "I like pruning" he said. My mother handed him the secateurs and left for town to get her hair done.

Mr Potterton -- in all the years that he worked for us I never knew his first name -- had a quite unique approach to gardening. It was only as you grew to know him -- everything except his first name that is -- that his approach to gardening made sense. Mr Potterton had no formal horticultural experience, no string of degrees or well thumbed diplomas. Mr Potterton assured us he had learned everything he needed to know about plants during the war. Which would have been all very well, had he perhaps spent the war in the home guard, helping dig for victory. But that was not the case. Mr Potterton had mostly been in Burma, fighting the Japanese. And his principal approach to the dense Burmese jungle had involved either a machete or a flamethrower, the choice ultimately depending on whether he anticipated Japanese snipers to be hiding behind the tangled creepers. As far as Mr Potterton was concerned, these techniques translated well to a domestic setting.

"I like pruning" turned out to be the understatement of the century. When my mother returned from the hairdressers, she barely recognised the back garden. Mr Potterton had clearly had a flashback. My mother had left a slightly overgrown but still obviously 1974 suburban garden. But to Mr Potterton, for whom the war had never really ended, this was a 1942 Burmese rainforest, riddled with Japanese sharpshooters and he had confronted his demons in the only way he knew how. To this day, I don't know where he found a machete.

As my mother stood aghast beside the smouldering embers of a bonfire the size of one of the Armada beacons, Mr Potterton emerged from behind the garage with the kind of 'anxious to please' look that made any rebuke pointless. Just then Charlie appeared on his scooter. "Where's the garden gone?" he asked.

Mother, always able to find the right words even in adversity, managed a wan smile. "Well at least it should be tidy now for the winter" she said.

It was only just April.

The awkwardness was broken by a loud pop. Charlie's football had somehow found its way into the bonfire.

My mother made a mental note never to leave cans of petrol in the garage. And also to insist that Mr Potterton did not bring his own tools to the house.

So for ten years, Mr Potterton was our gardener, an incredible span of time considering that, after a fortnight or two of his pruning, there was nothing much left to garden. Even simple gardening tasks were executed with a ruthlessness quite alien to 1970s suburbia. Nor did Mr Potterton pay any notice to seasonal rules. If he determined that the roses needed pruning, it mattered not one jot that the plants were heavy with blooms. Either way, they got the cold steel. One thing is for sure -- if there were any German or Japanese soldiers lurking in our garden before Mr Potterton, there certainly weren't any afterwards.

Thank goodness we never had foreign exchange students.

Somehow over the years I seem to have acquired many of Mr Potterton's characteristics, or at least his penchant for the sharper tools. My gardening mishaps are legion and stem largely from a pathological inability to distinguish weeds from plants. Particularly from expensive plants. If the garden is riddled with bindweed, I will unquestionably fail to notice. Moss all over the lawn? Well it's green isn't it. But a rare, exquisitely scented Peruvian orchid will draw the attention of my secateurs with the relentless accuracy of a cruise missile. Mr Potterton is long since gone but somehow his spirit seems to linger on in my own gardening.

And nowadays the tremors lend an additional frisson to the use of sharp tools in proximity to soft extremities. I'm sure the plants are thinking "one day ... one day soon". And they're probably right. Unlike Claire, with the green fingers, trowel-meister supreme and doyen of the hanging baskets, I am, a complete incompetent. My inability to recognise plants is perhaps understandable. After all, Mr Potterton saw to it that there were none more than a foot high in our garden. But if you ally that ignorance with an Olympic standard of general practical incompetence, and ever dwindling dexterity, the result is a heady brew of horticultural havoc. Not surprisingly, I have been relieved of the secateurs. My gardening forays are limited to mowing the lawn and cultivating herbs in pots. Not exactly 'full contact' gardening. I am in gardening terms, under house arrest.

Nor am I allowed near any new plants. A few weeks ago, for instance, we bought a rather beautiful young tree in a large pot with fragile crimson leaves. A Japanese Acer.

I can almost hear Mr Potterton drawing his machete. "Japs –did someone say Japs?

10th April 2010 ~ Trains

Railways are in my blood. My great great grandfather Tom, a Lincolnshire farm labourer, came to Doncaster in the 1850s, drawn by the newly opened Doncaster Locomotive Engineering Works and the many jobs available. For fifty years he worked in the Lower Turnery making railway carriages and locomotives. His son, also Tom, married the daughter of a Great Northern Railway engine driver and their son, my grandfather, (you've guessed it – Tom) started work there in 1917, just after his fourteenth birthday. For nearly a century my ancestors built trains in Doncaster for the nation's railways.

So I grew up loving trains and was lucky enough to catch the end of the steam age. Our house backed onto the London-Edinburgh line, that great artery of the London North Eastern Railway. I watched the big passenger trains, little shunters and goods trains that seemed to go on forever. Sometimes the guard would wave to me. I saw The Flying Scotsman pass by on its non-stop run. Each night, when my mother thought I was asleep, I would stand at the window in my pyjamas watching the big 4-6-2 expresses pass by, the orange glow from the fireboxes lighting up the night. I remember the first time I saw (and heard) one of the awesome new Deltics.

Many years later, when I worked in London, I would travel up to Cannon Street on what my wife called 'the gentleman's train' -- an ancient slam door, four carriage boneshaker that rattled its way from deepest Kent into London at a leisurely pace. It left just after nine and arrived on the dot of 10, too late to interest the commuters, yet too early to be eligible for cheap day returns. It was not a train for people in a hurry so much as a train for the aimless. It stopped everywhere, but for no apparent reason, since nobody boarded and nobody alighted. It was a local train for local people. My friend Trev the Train, a gentle giant of a man and a walking lexicon of local history and geography (and therefore your ideal Pub quiz partner) once told me with some authority that parts of its carriages dated back to the First World War. On the evidence of the trolley service, so did the ham sandwiches.

It seemed to be a forgotten train. When the rest of the Network Southeast's fleet of trains got their spanking new livery, the Train That Time Forgot received no such makeover. While the other trains were putting on airs and graces in their shiny blue and gold paintwork, the TTTF remained unfashionable but comfy, like an old baggy jumper. As comforting as slippers or a coal fire. No artificial voice announcements, no high-pitched whine of the electric motor, no digital signs enumerating every stop from there to Cannon Street.. Just ancient coachwork with the rich patina of beeswax and age, and big soft seats like trampolines. The TTTF even had its own smell -- the dust of an aged library, old cigars, and polish (for much of its coachwork was made of wood). And every day at exactly 9:04 AM, like EM Forster's celestial omnibus, it wheezed and rattled its way into the station.

Even at peak popularity, there would rarely be more than a dozen people per carriage. No babble of conversation, nor tinny iPod beats, only the occasional rustle of newspapers. It was more like a sleepy gentleman's club than a vital link in a modern rail infrastructure. Many times I would be alone in the carriage. On one occasion my only company was a pigeon who flew in through an open window at Sevenoaks. He hopped off at Orpington just as an inspector boarded -- I expect he didn't have a ticket.

Sadly the TTTF is no more. Inevitably some railway apparatchik must have finally asked why they were running the train and, presumably having never succumbed to its olde worlde charm, ran a red pen through its line in the timetable, thus ending nearly a century of rattling railway rambling.

I expect the TTTF is still meandering along an overgrown branch line somewhere. Old trains never die.

For someone who used to commute daily to London, I now travel as little as possible by rail. I left my job in London in 2003 and now only travel up for concerts or events. And each time I travel, I am left disappointed by the experience. The trains are plastic, overbrightly lit, and anonymous like a dentist's waiting room on wheels. Tom Stamford would not be impressed. Above all, the trains are crowded and passengers are rude and intolerant of the slow moving, such as myself. The last service at night from Charing Cross is less a train than a Bosch painting – redolent of madness and drunken menace. "Got any money mate?" I was once asked by a rather over-refreshed, belching Auk of a man. "Yes, thanks" I replied "but it's kind of you to ask". Only the laughter of other passengers prevented him from pursuing this line of inquiry with his fists. He laughed, bewildered but pleased with his joke, and, briefly distracted, lurched on his way. As did I, but for different reasons. And in the opposite direction.

But, whatever other deficiencies there may be, you can never level poor value against the railways. Only last month a few flakes of snow brought the network to a standstill. My train took nearly the entire evening to go from Waterloo to Tonbridge, inch by agonising inch. Was I downhearted? Of course not - where else in the world can you get four hours of travel for little more than a tenner?

17th April 2010 ~ Something for the Weekend

My brother Charlie and I shared a flat in London during the late 80s. In the corner of the living room was a cheap Portuguese television that periodically picked up non-terrestrial channels, police broadcasts and mobile phone conversations. Sometimes the Arts Show would be disrupted by snatches of "leave it 'aht guv'nor, You got nuffink on me" as The Bill briefly competed for the frequency band. On one occasion Charlie and I were transfixed when Emmerdale was interrupted by "In the event of a loss of cabin pressure, masks will drop down from the panel above you". We both looked up. In fact so erratic was the television's reception that it tended to be ignored. In any case, as young bachelors, we had better things to do with our time.

But, no matter how bad the reception, there were two programs each weekend that we watched religiously. Well religiously is the wrong word in the case of Blind Date. While Cilla is a national institution, many of the contestants on her program deserved to be in one. Week upon week they provided living proof of the hypothesis that the content and volume of speech are controlled by two wholly unrelated nerve centres. Each week a 'lucky' lad or lass got to take his pick from three candidates, the whole edifice underpinned by a baying studio audience

Because we the viewers could see the potential suitors, it was clear that Kevin should pick number 1, the softly spoken, statuesque blonde faintly reminiscent of Anita Ekberg. But it was equally certain that Kevin, separated from his quarry by a wall and thus oblivious to Anita's charms, would invariably plump for Sharon, the hypersexual narcissist and general sociopath. Like watching a train crash, it was horrible but strangely transfixing. And you could predict with equal certainty that their randomly-picked blind date would be a February weekend in Bognor rather than a fortnight in the Seychelles. Of course you had to come back the following week to find out just how miserable that date had been. Two egos into one tiresome weekend doesn't go.

In the end, Charlie and I used to drape a tea towel over the screen to add a frisson of excitement to proceedings. Suddenly we were Wayne, facing the same choices and fumbling for clues like the blinded Polyphemus. And inevitably, we picked Sharon over Anita every time. Sometimes Charlie added his own commentary "well Jon, you turned down number one, Anita a blonde lapdancer from Stockholm. And here is your blind date, Olga, a transsexual shot-putter from Vladivostok via Immingham."

A couple of beers and an hour of Blind Date were a perfect way to start a Saturday night. But eventually even this parade of the unsuitable failed to hold our interest. Because even in this theatre of the absurd, there was now something even more ridiculous. In 1993 the new kid on the block was Supermarket Sweep.

It's hard to believe that Dale Winton, the uncrowned king of the sunbed, started his illustrious TV career with a program called Supermarket Sweep. Even by the basement standards of TV in the early 90s, this was utter codswallop. In the same way that the face of King Priam's wife Helen launched the Greek fleet on their way to Troy, so did Dale Winton's mug launch Supermarket Sweep. And although the Trojans brought the war upon themselves, I'm still unclear what the television watching public had ever done to Dale Winton that called for retribution on the scale of Supermarket Sweep.

Still, for reasons I find hard to understand even now, Supermarket Sweep was, like Blind Date, gruesomely watchable. Hard to believe but apparently a seat in the studio audience was one of the hottest tickets available in the early 90s as Dale exhorted contestants to go wild in the aisles. I've often wanted to 'go wild in the aisles' as Dale would say, but for entirely different reasons. Never mind 'Dale's Display', I'm sure I could use the pricing gun to better effect.

In an interview many years later, Dale said that he thought one of the secrets to the show's success was his own 'sexual ambiguity' leaving viewers, he felt, wondering. Charlie and I clearly had a different definition of ambiguity. We had stopped 'wondering' within 15 seconds of the pilot show's titles. Charlie would even whistle the tune to YMCA.

And for many years Charlie and I attributed Dale's orange phizog to the Portuguese television, along with the limegreen snooker tables and luminous yellow beaches. It was only when I saw Dale at a charity event years later that I realised he actually was that colour. He had been well and truly Tangoed.

Nowadays I watch very little television. Which seems bizarre, considering the choice available. Where previously Charlie and I had usually found something worth watching from a mere four channels -- five if you count the flight attendant channel on the 6:55 PM Heathrow to Washington flight -- now we struggle to find decent entertainment from nearly 300 channels, all available at the flick of a switch or the tap of a button. Which is just as well really, because on particularly Parky days, that's about all I'm up to.

And you wouldn't believe the struggle for possession of the Sky remote. The remote control, like the stone of Scone, represents authority. The holder has the power to determine whether we watch an Eastenders bank holiday special or a 1947 Soviet propaganda film about cheesemaking in the Urals. Old Top Gear repeats or Bollywood pastiches. Operation TV or a shopping channel.

Only last week we lost the remote control. Or more accurately, we misplaced it. Family life as we know it ceased to exist. The children, brought up on a diet of after-school Hannah Montana, found themselves unable to change channels from BBC Parliament and, in their desperation, even resorted to inter-sibling conversation. Television has that power!

We found the remote by accident. Or more accurately Flora, the dog, found it. Rather than hand it over she tried to engage us in a tug of war. As she gripped it in her mouth, we were treated to a canine televisual rampage, flicking from parliament, international lacrosse, and the Top Gear 2007 Christmas special, to a gritty Northern documentary about two young scallywags dropping ketchup-filled condoms from the 18th floor of a Sheffield tower block onto cars below. Eventually, momentarily distracted by a second or two of Crufts, Flora surrendered the remote control - but not before a muddled and dislocating seque between Delia Smith, Gone with the Wind and the closing scene of Apocalypse Now.

"The houmous, the houmous".

"Frankly, my dear, I don't give a flan"

24th April 2010 ~ Teeth

Rather like an interrogation, I was tilted back in the chair with a bright light shone directly in my face and sharp metal instruments thrust in my mouth. All I could hear was "Upper right 8 buccal, lower right 6 occlusal, lower left 6 buccal occlusal..." And so it went on, a long litany of dental neglect, each new cavity greeted with a tut-tut from the dentist. In the end, the list of teeth requiring attention read like the names of the dead on a Somme War Memorial. Those teeth that did not have overt cavities were put 'on watch', rather like schoolchildren 'on report'. Perhaps that was it with my teeth - there was nothing inherently wrong, they just needed a good talking to and, quaking in their little roots, would buck their ideas up. A sort of ASBO for teeth.

But for some of my teeth it was already too late -- they had made their choices and chosen the path of cavities. For some of these enamelled recidivists, this was their second or third filling. These teeth had been up before the beak before and had not changed their ways. Too few apples and too many Crunchies. Way too many. My dentist delivered the verdict on my dodgy dentition. I half expected her to don the black cap, so grim was the news.... "You will be taken forth from here to a place of your extraction..."

I don't know what was worse, the reproachful look of the dentist and her assistant or the inevitable dental Armageddon that was to follow. I suggested to my dentist but perhaps there was no need to remove the teeth on the grounds that "I thought you were all into conservative dentistry" or "I or oo err aw i oo o err ah i en i ri" in the language of a man with his open mouth full of instruments and lignocaine. She obviously thought that I was making a joke because that's the only explanation I can find for the chimpanzee noises she made in reply. When the nurse joined in, I realised this was a well worked routine. Oh how I laughed.

Incidentally, why do dentists feel an urgent need to initiate conversations on complex metaphysical concepts only when your mouth is agape, and you're able to do little more than grunt. Yes and no are about as expansive a verbal repertoire as anyone can master in the dental chair. In the end, after a range of attempted communication methods including a sort of arm flailing semaphore and a variant of Morse (ah – aaaah – ah – ah – aaaaah), I managed to plea bargain the extractions down to mere fillings, with the promise of vastly more diligent dental hygiene in future. And at the time I said it, I meant it. In fact I even recall it being one of my New Year's resolutions last year. And the year before.

You would think that certain activities would be made easier by a natural tremor -- brushing my teeth being one of them. But in practice that isn't the case. I'm just as likely to brush my gums as my teeth. In fact the general inaccuracy of the brushing process usually results in the kind of white mouth reminiscent of Al Jolson. In any case, when the tremor is exacerbated by any stress, the up-and-down movements of brushing the front teeth run the risk of lodging a toothbrush in one of my nostrils.

In the bad old days of dentistry, some 50 odd years ago, teeth were regarded as something of an encumbrance. Something to go wrong. Perhaps not surprisingly, dentists tended to reach for the pliers rather than the drill. In fact my great aunt, had all her teeth extracted as a special 21st birthday present. Conservative dentistry before the First World War did not so much mean that you kept your teeth, as kept them in a jar. Not surprisingly over the years osteoporosis thinned her jaw to the point where she needed bone grafts. With hindsight, she would probably have preferred a car.

Even my mother had gaps where the dentist had clearly lost patience with her chalky teeth, and simply taken the path of least resistance. When my parents moved south from Yorkshire, they found a new dentist. My mother, always fearful of dentistry, engaged him in conversation, largely as a device to mask her inherent anxiety at the sound of the drill.

"I am told that teeth are the furniture of the mouth, Mr Rees" she said.

Mr Rees didn't even look up. "If that is so Mrs Stamford, you appear to have had the bailiffs in."

May

The fridge and more

1st May 2010 ~ The fridge

How many times have you shuffled downstairs in the middle of the night, and headed straight to the refrigerator? I'll also wager that you open the fridge, see nothing to eat and close it again. So what is it that drives you, thirty seconds later, to open the fridge again? What could possibly have changed in those thirty seconds? Perhaps that tired crumb of cheddar on the top shelf has somehow transmogrified into a ripe Stilton, rich with port? Or maybe a three-day-old chicken drumstick has become a baron of beef? Or have the cloudy dregs of the grape juice somehow been magicked into a 1982 Chateau Lafite?

Nope. None of that has happened. The cheddar is still dry and cracked, the drumstick greasy and unappealing. This is short-term memory failure at its most pronounced. Or perhaps at three in the morning we're just on autopilot. The same autopilot that lets us leave the house, get in the car, drive to the shops, buy a newspaper, drive back and turn the key in the lock without any recollection of any of the events in between. And don't say you haven't done it too, you fibber.

Back to the fridge – of course.

I've never really understood fridges. For some people, fridges are a groaning board, a horn of plenty, a muscular assertion of affluence, constantly restocked with goodies. For others the shelves are a finger-pointing indictment of our questionable eating habits When eyes are bigger than tummies, the resulting collateral damage finds its way to the refrigerator. If we're not sure what to do with something, we no longer throw it away. It goes in the fridge, a kind of purgatory for unwanted food. Neither consigned to oblivion in the bin, nor a happy heaven in our stomachs, it lurks unloved beneath the yoghurt. Neither one thing nor the other until eventually it will find its way into the bin. If it was unappetising to start with, days of chilling are not going to induce a sea change. Unless it's curry – a week in the slammer perks it up no end, in my view.

Nowhere is my theory about fridge contents more vividly illustrated than in the kitchen of a bachelor pad. Many years back, Charlie and I shared a flat in Paddington, two streets from the building where Sir Alexander Fleming had discovered penicillin. Our fridge reflected a certain dietary inexactitude, embodied by a style of cooking based principally around lager. Whilst many casseroles and stews are immeasurably enhanced by a slosh of red wine, hardly any are improved by lager. Yet Charlie and I persisted with our experimental off-piste cookery creating dishes that would have brought tears to the eyes of Escoffier. Believe me, liver curry is not for the fainthearted.

Since neither Charlie nor I would take responsibility for the fridge, it swiftly crossed over that Rubicon from repository of tasty morsels to third-year undergraduate microbiology project. I know precious little about moulds and fungi beyond what I have seen on the occasional slice of bread, or marbling stilton. But I'm pretty certain even from my limited knowledge, that red and yellow are bad colours to have in your fridge or, more accurately growing on things in your fridge. Green is almost respectable mould, dignified in a way - a return to nature perhaps. But red and yellow seem angrier and out of place in a fridge. Laboratory petri dish perhaps, but not a domestic refrigerator surely. Charlie said it looked like an MCC tie. Only Charlie could think of cricket when we were facing something from Quatermass, staring into a microbiological abyss even.

I even went as far as bringing home a book on identification of bacteria and fungi from the library. The book had many pictures of fungi in every shape form and colour imaginable – huge puffballs, Fly agarics, and the beautifully lyrical Trompettes de Mort. But strangely nothing that looked quite like the moulds growing on the second shelf behind the cottage cheese. The nearest match in the textbook seemed to be anthrax. I'm guessing it wasn't, because otherwise you wouldn't be reading this.

Only the other night, one of my sleepless rambles led me to the fridge door. For once, rather than reach for a piece of cheese, I took it upon myself to do a spot inventory. Sponge pudding, eggs, cheap sausages, Thai curry paste and so on. Of seventy nine separate items, twenty eight were outside their 'sell by' dates, in some cases so spectacularly so that they would have satisfied UN inspectors that we were in possession of biological warfare agents.

With the exception of highly perishable goods like chicken and fish, we have always taken a fairly bullish approach to sell-by dates, viewing that these are discretionary rather than mandatory. A week or so doesn't make much difference to an unopened pot of crème fraiche. A week in the life of a plate of offal however is an entirely different journey.

I lined up the out of date produce on the kitchen counter in order of days expired. Yes I know this is a tad obsessive but then we Parkies are known to be. Besides, it was 3am – what else is the Parkie insomniac to do? In last place, a mere two days expired, was a lone rasher of streaky bacon. But just as I was about to declare a winner, the jar of tahini more than two years out of date, something at the back of the salad crisper caught my eye. Like Dr Who and the Daleks I recognised my enemy. It was hard to say what it had once been because it was covered in vivid spots.

Of yellow. And red

8th May 2010 ~ Election Special

At the time of the last election, Catherine was a gawky 13-year-old in her second year at secondary school. While Tony Blair defeated Michael Howard and Charles Kennedy, Catherine was practising for her Grade 6 Flute, less interested in the contents of the ballot box than the contents of her knicker drawer. Now she is eighteen and not only can she vote, but she has. Blair, Howard and Kennedy are consigned to the dustbin of political history, replaced by Brown, Cameron and Clegg – different faces, same rosettes.

For the first time in ages, we have been talking politics at dinner, debating the merits of proportional representation, hung parliaments and whether that nice Mr Clegg looks better with a green or an orange tie. Weighty matters you understand and a departure from the usual table repartee. Normally politics is a taboo subject, considered unsuitable for the table chez Stamford, a par with gynaecological procedures and religion.

It has become apparent that the three voters in our house - Claire, Catherine and myself - are of a different political hue. And as the campaigns have developed, with television debates, appearances on chat shows and incessant baby kissing/pensioner hugging, firmly held opinions have swayed and tottered, like drunken divas in stilettos. When it came to the confines of the polling station, Claire hedged her bets, plumping for one party locally and another nationally. Catherine had no such electoral ambivalence, voting decisively for one party in both elections, with all the clarity of youth.

Funnily, the presence in the household of an elder sister now able to vote has engaged both Alice and Alex in election politics in a way that both their parents have so lamentably failed to do, if not always with predictable results. When your son asks you to outline the pertinent differences between UKIP and the Official Monster Raving Loony Party, it's not always possible to give a straightforward answer. A glib answer certainly but not necessarily an accurate one. It's probably just as well that twelve year olds don't vote.

So much is written about two party or three party politics that the majority of the electoral tapestry is largely ignored. It's a little-known fact (except those with Wikipedia) but there are in fact more than a hundred parties contesting the general election. Not all of them are contesting every seat mind you. But even so, there is clearly a vein of politics waiting to be tapped every five years. Even the Official Monster Raving Loony Party is now mainstream, dull and predictable even. Without the demented presence of Screaming Lord Sutch, a man who could wreak havoc in an empty room, their role as court jesters has been largely usurped by the likes of the Pirate Party UK or the Bus Pass Elvis Party.

A general disenfranchising of the electorate has presumably spawned the Best of a Bad Bunch Party and the No Candidate Deserves My Vote Party. I suspect the electorate would agree with them, and help them to lose their deposit. Even the Common Sense Party had enough of the aforementioned commodity to stand in only two constituencies. Which is more than can be said for the Magna Carta Party, which has thrown itself on the mercy of the electorate in no less than three constituencies. That's three lost deposits and £1500 down the toilet.

But the most remarkable of all is a party which proposes the most radical reform to the electorate since votes were given to women. Whilst we still retain a minimum age, currently 18, below which one cannot vote, there is no upper limit. As long as one is of sound mind, one can vote, vote and continue to vote as long as you live. But one party plans to extend that. CURE or, to give it its full name, Citizens for Undead Rights and Equality, plans to extend voting not to the dead -- that would just be dull and predictable -- so much as the undead. Standing on a platform of "zombies, like students, are people too", they have targeted four carefully chosen constituencies to build their power base - Brighton Pavilion, Twickenham, Hitchin & Harpenden and Doncaster Central.

They are clearly a force to be reckoned with because the day before the election, Ladbrokes were offering 201 to 1 against them winning the Brighton Pavilion seat. Exactly the same odds as they were offering for UKIP.

Spooky!

15th May 2010 ~ Tools

Wherever I go I carry an arsenal of tools with me – two penknives, two screwdrivers, wire stripper, reamer, hook, wood saw, chisel, metal file, metal saw, pliers, wire cutters and wire crimpers.

So what kind of person goes around with all these tools - OK, you're probably forming a mental image of me and my tools. Maybe you're thinking jeans, plaid shirt, steel toed boots and a toolbelt. If you're thinking toolbelt then you are also thinking Bob The Builder. Or the Village People. You're thinking huge cups of tea with five teaspoons of sugar.

Ah, but I also carry a magnifying glass, tweezers, pen, scissors, nailfile, and nail cleaner.

That's got you thinking. A manicurist maybe? A shy botanist preparing field samples for the microscope?

But even that's not an end to the cornucopia of hardware I sequester about my person. I can extract stones from a horse's hoof, trim its mane, and inspect its eyes for cataracts, before sawing wood and screwing together a new door for its stable.

If I had a horse, that is.

By any standards it is a lot of stuff. Hilary and Tenzing conquered Everest with less kit.

Most remarkably, I carry all of these in my trouser pocket. Ah, I hear you say, so you wear special trousers perhaps, with pockets the size of binbags, reinforced with kevlar? I leave the house looking as though I've inflated a barrage balloon in my underpants perhaps? No I do not jangle like a dustbin full of tin cans. Nor do I wear trousers the size of Pavarotti.

Of course you have all guessed by now -- I'm talking about a Swiss Army knife. If you had to think about Swiss contributions to world culture, the Swiss Army knife would be right up there with cuckoo clocks and alpenhorns. And maybe cowbells. And chocolate I suppose. There's probably other stuff I can't remember.

We talk about the knife culture nowadays as though it's something new. But when I was young, all boys carried penknives. Not for filleting each other or other random acts of violence, but because the penknife was essential for all those things that young boys had to do to while away the decades before the Wii or Xbox were invented -- like sharpening sticks, and carving your initials on trees. Boy stuff. Outdoor stuff.

All gone now -- we have traded the cuts and grazes of youth for childhood obesity and juvenile diabetes as a generation of blubbery misanthropic kids exercise no more than their thumbs. No penknives, no daylight, no fresh air.

I'm rambling as usual. But my point is that penknives were not the province of homicidal maniacs, so much as a simple part of growing up. And the kids who had Swiss Army knives were the envy of all. It was like your dad owning an Aston Martin. Serious playground credibility!

All of which leads me to ponder whether we're talking about the knife of the Swiss Army or an Army knife of the Swiss. Does it matter? At this point many of the readers are skipping a paragraph or two, thinking not unreasonably that an outbreak of pedantry is imminent, and seeking to quarantine themselves from a Lynne Truss moment. For the record, it is the former. Victorinox actually do make knives for the Swiss Army. All of which came as a bit of a surprise to me because it never crossed my mind that this ultra-pacifist nation would have an army. And in any case why? I couldn't tell you when the last Swiss act of aggression was perpetrated. And being neutral, they have been spectators rather than participants in most 20th-century history.

You could probably tell all of that from the Swiss Army knife. This is not a nation hell-bent on world domination, with a belligerent sabre-rattling militia. This is a reluctant sleepy army. They probably wear camouflaged slippers...

The first Swiss Army knife, invented in 1891, had a couple of blades and that was that. But with a little bit of mechanical jiggery-pokery, they succeeded in creating space for more tools. It speaks volumes about the Swiss Army that the first additional tool chosen was the corkscrew. Not a splinter extractor, razor, saw or hammer. No, it was a corkscrew. Forgive me if I seem ungracious but I can't help but form the impression that the Swiss Army was not planning on doing much fighting. No daring dawn raids into enemy territory. Reveille in the Swiss Army was accompanied less by the sound of rifles being cocked than bottles being uncorked. Less bang than pop. And you thought "an army marches on its stomach" was a figure of speech.....

My Swiss Army knife was a present from Claire, my wife (or fiancee as she then was). It had 40 tools and cost £40. And that was 25 years ago, when £40 would buy a moderately equipped hatchback or make an adequate down payment on a three-bedroom semi in Surbiton.

All the knives have names. Mine was called "The Scientist" and, since I was one, seemed a sensible choice. Ok it wouldn't run Southern blots, separate molecular stereoisomers or split the atom, but it did pretty much everything else. Unlike "The Stockbroker" which did nothing at all but came with a villa in Tuscany and a yacht in Antibes. OK I'm fibbing – there was a corkscrew.

Of course Victorinox have moved with the times. Whereas before it was all screwdrivers, nail files and corkscrews, the new generation of Swiss Army knife (presumably for a new generation of Swiss soldiers) has memory sticks, digital watches, and torches. There is one entitled the Presentation Master which caught my eye. A mere eight tools – blade, nailfile with screwdriver, scissors, key ring, laser pointer, Bluetooth® and a 32 GB memory stick. In fact the single blade is all that qualifies it for the description of Swiss Army knife at all. Clearly the modern Swiss Army spends its entire life in a vortex of PowerPoint. No daily trench digging, no whiff of cordite, no stretcher bearers, nothing. Just a USB fitting to connect your knife to the computer and download your presentation. Everything you need is there - a laser pointer to highlight the key features of each slide, a screwdriver to rewire the projector, a nail file to while away the hours spent listening to other people's presentations and of course the knife for sharpening sticks or dealing with the more insistent hecklers.

The Presentation Master even has a fingerprint module. So now the knife will let you apprehend villains, read them their rights, and even fingerprint them. Then, for hardened criminals, you can always subject them to your PowerPoint presentation on "New developments in fast flow kettle nozzles", although on reflection that's probably banned under the Geneva Convention.

The Geneva Convention. There you go -- I knew there was something else.

25th May 2010 ~ What is a blog?

I don't think I write a blog at all.

Let me explain. After all, when I started this last September, one of the first questions I asked -- rhetorically and on your behalf as it were -- was who am I and why would you want to read anything I wrote? Eight months on, I'm still trying to answer the same question. More to the point, I have signally failed to establish even whether you read anything I wrote, let alone why that might be the case.

But I am helped here by the Wobbly Williams Webmeister who provides me with all kinds of information about who visits the website.

For instance, Mrs Muriel Trimble of 73 Acacia Avenue, Stoke Poges reads the blog while she is cooking spaghetti

Bolognese for the children, watching reruns of Dad's Army on UK TV Gold, while Stan Bartlett, a tenant farmer from Dumfries reads the blog in his landrover whilst taking a break from shearing his sheep.

I have visions of Gareth, like Blofeld, stroking his white cat and charting Wobbly Williams world domination with a fiendish laugh.

Mwah ha ha.

OK, the stats aren't as detailed as that – this is Wobbly Williams not the CIA – but they do tell me the basics. So I know not just how many people read the blog, but also where they read it. In the broadest sense, you understand -- the stats will tell me the general location (country or state) and times and dates of the Slice of Life hits.

On the face of it it's encouraging -- the stats suggest that several hundred of you in cyberspace read the blog each week. Most readers are British -- or at least located in the UK -- which is probably not surprising, since I write in English and much of the subject matter is parochial. Perhaps more surprising – to me at least – is the number of readers I have around the world. A few readers in the USA and Canada is understandable but how about the tiny but loyal handful of readers I have in Russia, China, and Croatia. And can I say a big welcome to my single reader in Latvia!

Well I say readers, but actually I can't even say that -- several hundred click on the Slice of Life page and stay there for a minute or so but does that mean you read it? Perhaps you go and make a cup of tea, just to fool me. And the Webmaster, sat in his swivel chair stroking the cat.

An old friend of mine, many years ago, submitted his PhD thesis and turned up to the oral examination with a bottle of whisky. He placed the bottle on the table beside him, without explanation, and opened his thesis. On conclusion of the viva 3½ hours later, the lead examiner asked him to explain the bottle of whisky. Steve invited them to turn to Page 256 and read out line 17. It read "the bottle of whisky is a prize for the first examiner to draw attention to this sentence". None of the three examiners won. And it is probably just as well that Steve waited till after the viva before insulting his examiners. It was probably just as well. The examiners, on seeing the whisky, had misinterpreted its presence as a gesture of premature triumphalism and, in consequence, had submitted Steve to an altogether more robust examination and was otherwise warranted.

So who am I writing for? And why?

As I think I said in my very first blog, this is not a format with which I have much experience. In reading other people's blogs, I find that I don't always follow the rules. I get the impression that most people feel a blog is closest to a diary. And that worries me. Because all my diaries were written when I was a teenager and there is a danger of turning into Adrian Mole (aged 52¾).

At its worst, a blog can be little more than a catalogue of meals, television, the kids' days at school, and domestic tittle tattle. A diary of the very worst sort, and probably not even of interest to immediate family members let alone those who've never met me. You don't want to read that any more than I want to write it -- I think. Only Garrison Keillor can carry off that sort of thing, turning home spun whimsy into engaging, life affirming parables.

Okay so diaries are out. And despite a love for the work of Keillor, I know my limitations. So I looked around the other writing models. Do I simply want to tell you about Parkinson's? About what it's like to live with this condition? Certainly that is a part of it, but it's only part of the story. In any case, shakes, stiffness and slowness may be a leitmotiv but, even for other Parkies, that can be a big yawn.

A long-standing family friend, and godmother to my sister, writes for the Guardian -- indeed many say she is the only reason to read the Guardian. Her work is unfailingly entertaining, distilling the banal to short shots of penetrating prose. She is one of a tiny handful of writers who can make me laugh aloud. Bill Bryson is another.

In the end they showed me the way and I thought that I would focus on one simple task – to make you laugh. After all PD is not without its funnier moments so let's enjoy them.

In the words of Irving Berlin:

There may be trouble ahead
But while there's moonlight and music
And love and romance
Let's face the music and dance

30th May 2010 – Friends

We were in Carluccio's. Anton and I had been watching the lads play cricket on the Sunday morning and we had arranged to meet the girls in the pub for lunch afterwards.

The game had overran and the pub was no longer serving food. Ten past two on a Sunday – is it too much to ask?

Perhaps the owners were rushing off to church or needed the pub for a local prayer group? Not a bit of it. They just don't do food after two and rules is rules. Never mind that there were ten of us, all hungry and ready to eat heartily, with bulging wallets ready to discharge their contents .They could stay in business for another week. It's not rocket science so much as basic economics. You have food to sell -- I want to buy food -- you sell me food. But no, not a bit of it. Rules is rules. Apparently beer, pork scratchings and fiscal oblivion are preferable.

So we decamped to Carluccio's en famille, just as it started to rain. No time limits. No restrictions. If it was on the menu, we could have it. We ordered drink. I had a lemon granita having recklessly squandered my two units on Harveys IPA in the pub. The girls, who were not driving, were making light work of the house rose.

I was fiddling around with the olives, debating whether to toss one skyward and catch it in my mouth (rarely successful even before PD) when a raised eyebrow from Claire made it clear that this was not a good example to set the younger children. Or adults for that matter. Out of the corner of my eye, I could see Alex, bread roll in hand, ready to shout "Food Fight!"

"You know I'm Swiss" said Freia. I looked up and nodded. "Well I've a bone to pick with you".

It was probably the Harveys because, for the life of me, I couldn't see what being Swiss had to do with olives.

Nothing actually, as it emerged. The gist of Freia's grievance was that, throughout a previous blog on the Swiss Army Knife I had neglected to mention her

Swissliness. Oops. Mind you, in my litany of things Swiss, I also forgot to mention the huge Swiss stockpiles of anthrax but I don't see anyone complaining about that.

Okay I accept that Freia is one of Switzerland's better exports. But the truth is I don't really think of Freia as Swiss although I freely concede that her signature dish of Geschnetzeltes and Rosti should perhaps have alerted me to the fact she was not from round these parts. But I'm a man. We don't notice much.

Woman (to husband): "Notice anything different about me?"
Man (looks up from newspaper) "New hairdo?"
Woman: "No. Try again"
Man: "New lipstick?"
Woman: "Try again"
Man: "New mascara?"
Woman: "No, I'm wearing a gasmask"

Anyway, for the record, let it be known that Freia is Swiss. As Swiss as a Swiss Army Knife. Or Gruyere. Or a cuckoo clock. All of which means that Tom, her son, is therefore eligible for military service in 10 years time and goodness knows what the Swiss Army Knife will look like by then.

Actually I am not sure Tom should be allowed knives if Anton, his dad, is anything to go by. Opposable thumbs have evolved over millennia to distinguish men from apes. But one misguided moment opening a paint tin with the aforementioned weapon all but reversed 3 million years of evolution for Anton. And nearly ended his cricket season before it had begun.

It's probably better that the Swiss are pacifists. They're a danger to themselves.

Joking aside, Freia and Anton are great friends of ours – kind, supportive and always entertaining. Freia is trying to talk Claire into a bank breaking extension to the house. I am retaliating by subliminally persuading Anton to buy a Jag. Well, not so subliminally really. We appear to be running a race to see which family can bankrupt the other first. A bit like Monopoly in reverse. Speaking as a tightfisted Yorkshireman, there's only going to be one winner.

But pasta solves everything. By the end of the meal, dipping biscotti into a glass of Vinsanto, Freia had forgotten she was Swiss, I was forgiven, and the weekend was winding down to a boozy close. Homework to finish, schoolbags to pack...whatever. I fell asleep on the sofa. "Lightweight" said Freia, unimpressed.

But the weekend had not started auspiciously. Clowning around in the nets, Tom had somehow clouted Alex across the shoulder with a cricket bat. Of course Alex shouldn't have been there in the first place. "Knock for knock" is what insurance companies would say. Although Alex and Tom are besties much of the time, the mood in the car between the two of them was decidedly frosty on the way home. Alex was still sulky the following morning when his shoulder prevented him bowling in the match. Still that's the thing with friends -- you can't stay angry. A plate of lasagne later, they were as thick as thieves again, and hatching some detailed plot on a napkin, to somehow elicit maximum discomfiture from their sisters.

So what are friends and how do you define them? The Oxford English dictionary is decidedly circumspect, offering "people between whom the state of friendship exists" or somesuch monumentally unhelpful circumlocution. But the more you think about it, the more difficult it is to pin down. I think the easiest functional definition of a friend is someone for whom you would give more than you take. They can be next door or on another continent. They can be people you see hourly or once in a decade. They are people who have marked your life in ways which have made you a better person. They have seen you at your worst and at your best and treat each the same.

They are people for whom time stands still.

I answered the phone the other day. "Are you coming to the bash on Saturday?".said Rollo

"Of course we are" I said, picking up the conversation from where we had left it when we last spoke. Two years earlier, that was.

Like I said, time stands still.

June

Thermodynamics

8th June 2010 ~ Fat

I am fat.

There, I said it. And that's the first step. Before you can address any problem, you have to admit that there is a problem. I have and there is. In the bathroom the other day, I took a long hard look at the man in the mirror. And I didn't like what I saw. In fact I didn't even recognise what I saw. For years I thought I saw the same man as always. Like the Hall of Mirrors at a funfair, the mind somehow distorts what is really there, flattering and misleading. Somehow I never spotted the waistline that was expanding as fast as my hair was receding. Perhaps I didn't want to see it.

But the bathroom mirror was speaking clearly enough. It wasn't saying "Hey, good looking" so much as "Oi, blubberbutt -- yes I'm talking to you". And it hasn't just been the mirror – the kids have clearly seen it too. "Dad, you're a bit of a chunky monkey these days" Catherine said to me over breakfast last week. And that is about as diplomatic and kind as it got. "Flabalanche!" shouted Alex yesterday, as I ran down the stairs to answer the phone. "Am I getting fat?" I asked Alice. "Wrong tense Dad" snorted Alice, continuing to file her nails. Brutal but honest.

There have been other signs. Like the creaky stairs. It was only last week that I realised the stairs only creaked when I walked on them. And all those jumpers that had mysteriously 'shrunk in the wash'. Apparently not.

"Never mind – you still have the body of a god" says Claire giggling "Buddha, that is".

Very funny.

So it's official – I am fat. In the eyes of my family, monstrously obese. Awash with adiposity. Positively piling on the pounds. Buoyant with blubber. I'm not sure it's as bad as that but the BMI needle is certainly into the red zone.

So let's not shilly-shally or skirt around the point with bland euphemism or hackneyed circumlocution. I am not "well padded", "stout" or "chubby". The word is fat - a porker. At 5' 9", I can't even delude myself I am 'big-boned', that risible refuge of those in terminal denial. A stegosaurus has claim legitimately to be big-boned, but not me.

Weight gain is a common enough problem in Parkinson's. It's not surprising really – as mobility decreases, we expend less energy. The long countryside walks with the dog become brief stumbles and shuffles to the postbox. Cycles to the shops become drives to the shops. And bit by bit we realise we are no longer taking as much exercise as we should. Energy input greater than expenditure and the result is weight gain. It's not rocket science.

So naturally we adjust our diet to match it. Less exercise means less food, right.

Er... wrong actually.

I can't speak for you but I have to admit that I am more sinner than saint when it comes to food. A salad dodger. "No thanks" always seems to come out as "Yes please". But to be honest I've always enjoyed food. Despite a lifelong dislike of celery and tomatoes, I've usually found something in the cupboard I wanted to eat. As Claire says, I graze rather than eat. And the consequences of this are catching up with me now.

Don't get me wrong -- this has not been a 50-year burgerfest. Nor have I been down the chippy every Friday night for fried Mars bars or standing alongside Gazza at the kebab van. And I only ever have a full English breakfast about once a decade. But I do have to admit a certain penchant for gnocchi à la Gorgonzola, Penne al Pesto, and most Italian desserts.

It wasn't always thus. As a lad, I was so skinny that nothing fitted me. Shop assistants would run the tape measure over me twice, convinced they had mismeasured. Mother was forever taking my trousers in at the waist. I remember her with the Singer on the kitchen table, slashing great acres of cloth out of my new C&A strides.

I looked like the starving children in the posters for Biafran famine relief. As a ten year old, my party piece for visitors was to lift my shirt and breathe in deeply, thus revealing a rack of ribs like a xylophone. "Honestly, he eats plenty" my mother would say by way of explanation.

I was fond of performing the same trick for patients visiting my father's surgery. While my father ministered to the sick and needy, I would sit at the top of the stairs and greet new patients as they arrived. "They're starving me" I would say, before treating them to the full octave on the xylophone.

But that was more than 40 years ago and you would struggle to recognise xylophone boy in the man I am now. The xylophone is now a kettle drum. The rack of ribs is now more a self-basting turkey.

Partly this has been a gradual process, assisted by the odd Crunchie here and there. And for the most part, the weight gain has gone unnoticed. I've never been one of those people who checks my weight daily on the bathroom scales. In fact I don't really think about weight at all. But the other day, I was conducting the usual summer triage of my wardrobe, separating the fashion disasters from the timeless style. Not that I have much of either, always being conservative in my clothing. No, you will find no mankini there. No Day-glo lycra lurking in my undergarments.

More than usual however, there seemed to be disproportionate number of garments that still had plenty of wear left but somehow no longer fitted me. As someone who seems to affect a sort of tramp chic (according to the wife), this is unusual. Mostly my garments wear out. But this summer, the clothes we're a damning indictment of my expanding girth as zips failed to zip and buttons ricocheted round the room. Squatting to pick up a sock, there was an unmistakable tearing sound from below decks so to speak, as another pair of trousers bit the dust. There comes a point in time when one has to accept that one is never going to wrestle the flabdomen into those 34 inch waist trousers again.

Sometimes the process of acceptance is easy -- you shrug your shoulders and buy the next size up. Yet somehow, like surrendering the things of youth, this can be surprisingly difficult. But I am tired of being Thor the Buffet Slayer. It's time for action.

7th June 2010: 14 stone 3 pounds. A line in the sand.

Well, more of a trench really.

25th June 2010 ~ Chaos

The Second Law of Thermodynamics states that all systems tend towards a maximum state of entropy. Put simply, things get messier and more chaotic. Mostly the law is applied to biological systems and is used to explain decay to recalcitrant GCSE students. But it applies to other structures in equal measure. Nobody with teenage children would doubt the general applicability of the law for a second. For Catherine, Alice and Alex, their bedrooms are living embodiments of the Second Law of Thermodynamics. In fact, there must be a special application of the law to knickers.

With three teenagers in the house (Alex turned 13 this week -- more on that another time), the bedrooms have acquired the character of an archaeological dig, with clearly defined strata. I vaguely recollect that the carpet in Alice's room was beige but it's been so long since I've seen it. And as for Catherine's bed, Tracy Emin would clearly identify a kindred spirit. As her father however, I'm a tad less impressed by the sweet wrappers and empty pizza box among the packages waiting to go off to their lucky eBay recipients. Alex's room looks like the set of a Mad Max film, with bits of broken spaceships and racing cars nestling among strange hybrid creatures, demonstrating what an overfertile imagination can do with old teddy bears, Barbie dolls, superglue and glow in the dark paint. It's not Blue Peter as I remember it anyway.

But it is a practical example of the Second Law of Thermodynamics.

The problem is that we are hoarders, a family of squirrels. I lose track of the number of times objects have been consigned to the loft on the specious grounds that they "might come in useful". They don't. More to the point, if they weren't useful when you put them in the loft how precisely are they meant to acquire some new sense of purpose buried under old newspapers? There are items in the loft which we haven't seen in 15 years, when they were last moved from the loft in the previous house. If these were part of a national archive, or items of astonishing value, it might be understandable. But with the best will in the world, chairs missing legs, chipped vases, small balls of string, old leather briefcases and bulbless torches oozing battery gel are not high on the V&A's wish list.

So we've been having a bit of a clear out recently. This week, as GCSEs are consigned to history -- until August that it is -- I suggested that they might like to use the opportunity to clear out some of the old toys and so forth. Their initial reluctance magically abated when I handed them a black bin liner each and suggested that if they didn't fill it I would. Alice realised I meant business when I shovelled a handful of lipsticks and mascaras into the bag. I've never seen her get out of bed so fast. Come to think of it, Catherine and Alex shifted pretty briskly as well, anticipating that I might mete out the same retribution on their caves.

All credit to them, they applied themselves to the task with an enthusiasm hitherto absent from their domestic endeavours. Out went broken toys, clothes too tatty to pass on, old cassette players, electronic games, and the kind of bric-a-brac that only children retain. And incidentally I can confirm that you Alice's carpet is indeed beige. Well mostly -- apart from the bits where the Parker pen had disgorged its contents. And the spot where the dog, as a puppy, had done the same.

To be honest I was glad to see it all go. But I've always had a weak spot for books. Perhaps because I write for a living, words are important and books -- all books -- are precious, things to be cherished. So when the kids started piling old redundant books on the landing, images of Nazi book burnings filled my mind.

Interspersed among the copies of King Lear and Jane Eyre – yes I know you thought they were hidden Alice – was an entire library of children's books. And a complete set of Letterland although that is probably not a series I get misty eyed over. In any case the books will go to the hospice shop.

The cleaner was mightily impressed. For the first time in ages she could deploy the Hoover to its intended purpose without pausing every few seconds to pull earrings, exam notes and biscuits from its hungry maw. "It's all thermodynamics" I said, before treating her to a detailed explanation of the principles.

She listened patiently while I dwelt on the nuances of enthalpy, entropy and free energy, nodding sagely as I pontificated at length on the myriad applications of the science. "Any questions?" I ended finally.

"Yes" she said "where's the bleach?"

July

Indoors, outdoors and blue doors

4th July 2010 ~ Euphemism, understatement and circumlocution

I make no bones about it, I have always enjoyed wordplay. Hyperbole, simile, satire -- it's all grist to the mill. But my favourites are circumlocution, understatement and euphemism. The English language is too rich not to take the scenic route. Why go from A to B directly when C and D are nearby and just as interesting. And the British gift for finding some good in everything underpins our use of euphemism. Above all, I love the derivation of words. Mostly Latin or classical Greek, but common roots underpin so many modern words. I am, if you will, a man who believes in calling a spade a geotome.

I blame my school. More specifically, I blame Mr Hugo, my Latin teacher who owned a chateau in the Loire and only taught in order to pay for its upkeep. An agonisingly erudite man who would crack jokes in Latin and then be crestfallen when none of his charges had the slightest idea what he was talking about. Invariably some clod, usually one of the DeVere brothers would ask whether there was likely to be an exam question on it, which temporarily brought Mr Hugo down from the intellectual stratosphere. Sometimes his explanations of the jokes would also be in Latin. And if in particularly playful mood, he would summon some ink-covered unfortunate from the back row of desks to effect a simultaneous translation of Homer or Virgil. Usually DeVere minor.

He revelled in language, in its rhythm and meter, eschewing the grey and mundane in favour of vivid, evocative mouthfuls. Our progress in Latin was not 'slow' but 'testudinarious'. The raven haired Penelope Craddock was not 'pretty' so much as 'pulchritudinous'. And even when two boys had evidently copied their homework from each other, there was no hint of 'foul play' -- only 'skulduggery'.

But his tongue could just as easily be used to cut. Although he did not outwardly resent people less intelligent than himself – which was pretty much everyone – he had no truck with those who affected the Luddite bearing of teenagers. He was frequently blind to honest endeavour, seeing merely the mask of fecklessness. He took particular exception to the PE staff, regarding them all as grunting Neanderthals. After one egregiously uncomfortable lunch with a teacher that even the PE department referred to as Monkey, he was heard muttering that he had just wasted half an hour 'in the presence of a man who would make a gatepost seem like Euclid'. And I don't think he was talking about lorries.

Although not noted for his use of hip euphemism, he would doubtless have recognised Monkey as an experiment in artificial stupidity. Certainly Monkey had an intellect is only rivalled by garden tools. More than a few clowns short of a circus, even Darwin would have been satisfied that Monkey was evidence that evolution also had a reverse gear. Monkey's facial hair was so extensive that not only did his eyebrows meet in the middle, they extended as far as his ears. Certainly he lent weight to the recent finding by geneticists that we -- well humanity in general -- share 70% of the same genetic information as watercress. For Monkey, it may have been more.

Mr Hugo is long since gone, a victim of Parkinson's, diagnosed at a time when treatment options were few and endurance shorter. During the 5 years I was at school his stride became a shuffle, his copperplate script became spider scrawl, and ready smile became a frozen sneer as the PD mercilessly stole the power of expression from a man to whom expression was everything.

Monkey too is gone, a dinosaur unable to adapt as teaching changed - a book permanently out of print, roadkill on the information superhighway, with reservations at the Chateau Eternity, winning one for the Reaper.

But Mr Hugo left me with a love of euphemism. As Quentin Crisp once said "euphemisms are unpleasant truths wearing diplomatic cologne". Some are just plain dull -- we don't die, we pass away. Actors are not unemployed but resting. Drunken friends are over refreshed. Perhaps the most dramatic understatement of the 20th century was that of Emperor Hirohito. When he spoke to Japan on 14 August 1945, after two nuclear bombs had razed Hiroshima and Nagasaki, he explained that 'the war situation has developed not necessarily to Japan's advantage'.

I'll say.

Nowhere are euphemisms more rampant than in politics and International relations -- why tell barefaced lies when you can simply be 'economical with the truth'? And where can 'my honourable friend' be my bitterest enemy? And who would ever use torture instead of 'enhanced coercive interrogation techniques'? And 'special rendition' sounds so much nicer than kidnapping

But like Mr Hugo, I'm generally intolerant of cliche euphemisms. When guests ask me where they can 'powder their nose', I always tell them that we have a strict anti-drugs policy in this house. If they request directions to 'the smallest room in the house', they usually find themselves in the wine cellar. When they want 'the little boy's room', I tell them we don't have one -- Alex is a teenager. If they express a desire to 'wash their hands', I happily take them to the kitchen sink.

Yes I know it's childish but we all have to get our laughs somehow.

Claire constantly tells me to behave "this is why we are losing friends" she says.

I'd better end with a joke.

Puer: Cur hi homines, pater, currunt?
Pater: Certant de argenteo calice
Puer: Et quis accipiet?
Pater: Primus
Puer: Cur igitur ceteri currunt?

Oh, you've already heard it...

11th July 2010 ~ Grandmas

For the first 10 years of my life I had two grandmothers, and you would struggle to find two more different grannies. Grandma Blue Door, a gentle birdlike artist, lived in a small bungalow with a long strip of rose-bordered garden that backed onto the town fields. She would wave to me from the bottom of her garden when I was playing football on the fields, during school games. "I never knew grandma was interested in football" I said to my mother. "She isn't" she replied "but she likes to see her grandson". So, at half-time, I would wander over to the fence with my slice of orange in my mouth and pull faces to make her laugh. She would reward me with barley sugars. Sometimes our grey-haired games master, Mr Latham would talk to my grandma in French and they would giggle and cast furtive glances at me.

Grandma George was a different kettle of fish. A fierce overbearing matriarch who lived in a huge Gothic detached house with a fish pond and artificial streams. We would go round to her house on Sunday afternoons where we ate chicken with Yorkshire pudding followed by my favourite desserts for 10 years -- my aunt Kath's lemon meringue pie, sweet yet mouth-puckeringly sharp at the same time. In summer we would play in the garden among the pampas grass, and fashion fishing rods out of bamboo canes and parcel twine. In winter we made a den in the living room under grandma's baby grand. At 5 PM, still bloated from overindulgence at lunch, we would face high tea -- slices of ham, boiled eggs, and little cakes or 'fancies' as my grandma called them. Grandma George was a self-made woman, having run a haulage business for decades. Unsurprisingly she held strong views on many subjects, but nothing lit her fuse more than the Labour Party and immigration. And in the privacy of her own home, with what she perceived to be a receptive audience, she would hold forth, spewing eye-wateringly robust opinions unchallenged during the advert breaks in 'I Love Lucy', what passed for comedy on Sunday evening in the 1960s. Fierce she was, but also fiercely protective and with a fondness for her grandchildren that, with Yorkshire stoicism, she felt keenly but rarely articulated.

I had no grandfathers. Fred, Grandma Blue Door's husband had died many years before I was born, his health never having recovered properly from the First World War. He was gassed on the Somme and wounded at Passchendaele. Although I have no recollection of him, we have his medals and many postcards from the Western front. And we have photographs of him, standing jauntily in the queue to enlist in 1915, and again in 1919 in a demob suit, with wan smile and haunted eyes that betrayed the horrors of the trenches. Grandma George was widowed in 1940. Tom, a wild man by any standard, brimming over with self destructive impulse, met his maker aged 37. His gravestone read 'now in God is keeping, safe and at rest'. She took the name George from her current beau, or rather we her grandchildren assigned it to her.

My own children distinguished their grandparents from each other by location. There was 'Nanna Up the Road ' who lived a few streets away and Nanna North who lived, or more accurately had lived, in Yorkshire. Strangely, although she lived in Sussex for the last 15 years, the name stuck. And so she remained Nanna North until near the end of her life when, taking heroic doses of morphine to keep the pain at bay, Alice used to sometimes address her affectionately as Nanna Smack. Nanna's husband, my father, eschewed Grandpa, Grandad or Gramps in favour of GwaGwa.

It would take too long to explain. Really it would.

Grandparents are important. Although we saw my grandmothers a lot when I was young, each visit was still special. The love of grandparents for their grandchildren is wonderfully free and irresponsible. As Ogden Nash said 'When grandparents enter the door, discipline flies out the window'. True. It wasn't my mother who bought me gobstoppers so big you couldn't speak. It was Grandma Blue Door. And it wasn't my father who gave me a gulp of Advocaat. It was Grandma George. And when Grandma George said 'don't tell your father', you didn't.

Not only have my grandchildren had a full quota of grandparents, they even had a great grandmother who chose to be known as 'Grandma', thereby pulling rank on the mere Nannas. Not Grandma This or Grandma That. Just Grandma. On Wednesday mornings she would look after Catherine, our only child at that time, while Claire went shopping. When she returned, Catherine would be happy and gurgling with contentment. She loved going round to Grandma's. Not surprising too -- Grandma had this theory that honey cleansed the palate and was antiseptic. So just before Claire returned from shopping, Grandma would feed Catherine a spoonful of lavender honey. No wonder she gurgled with contentment. All the kids loved her and, even in the nursing home, Grandma thrived on visits from my boisterous trio.

As Sam Levenson once said, the reason grandparents and grandchildren get along so well is that they have a common enemy.

16th July 2010 ~ The sporting life

Parkies need exercise so on summer Saturday afternoons I play cricket.

Well I say 'play' but this is probably too strong a word. Mainly what I do is stand like a jelly statue in whites at gully, hands cupped in anticipation of the catch which will inevitably fly past me like the Tokyo bullet train, for four. If the ball actually does make contact with any part of my body, the likelihood is that it will be my belly (simply on the law of averages, since it occupies the largest part of my frame), or crotch (as the most delicate part of me). The probability of a catch landing in my hands, and sticking there, are approximately 1 divided by Avogadro's number. The team are resigned to my many fielding failures. "Like a gazelle, Jon" calls our Aussie wicket-keeper -- a dead ringer for Phil Jupitus incidentally - as I misfield another shot and land upside down in a crumpled heap. "Never mind Jon, it was a tough chance" is the wearied response of fielders too polite to point out that I'm actually still wearing my reading glasses, after my stint as scorer.

When I bat it's not much better.

The best batsmen -- the Kevin Pietersens and Brian Laras of this world - talk about shot selection -- the rapid mental cogitation and choice of a stroke appropriate to the delivery the batsman is facing. Shot selection requires two things of the batsmen -- a very good eye and an arsenal of shots from which to choose. For the top batsmen, that is a given. I, on the other hand, have the eye of Horatio Nelson and when it comes to the range of my shots, images of bare shelves in pre-glasnost Soviet supermarkets come to mind. Quality batsmen decide which strokes to play as the ball leaves the bowlers hand. Usually I have made my mind up before the bowler has walked back to his mark. In actual fact, like all the great batsmen, I have many shots in my locker. It's just that, in my case, that's where they stay.

Like my fielding, my batting bewilders team mates. Comments like "Jon is not picking the googly" might suggest, to the casual observer, that this is the sole deficiency in an otherwise peerless technique. In actual fact "Jon is not picking the googly" is only the first part of a larger unspoken sentence that continues "or the flipper, the doosra, the arm ball, the inswinger, the outswinger, the bouncer, or the Yorker". A litany of cricketing ineptitude.

The team have long since relinquished any lingering hope of a Stamford fifty and recognise that any innings will be brief. I usually walk out to bat not to a ripple of applause so much as the sound of the kettle being filled. My 'signature stroke' (a polite euphemism for 'only stroke' if the truth be told) is the wild mistimed pull through mid-wicket. This is applied universally, irrespective of the length or line of the delivery. At least my batting is uncomplicated. Short, wide, full or straight, it is addressed with the same shot. Only the outcome differs. Either way, the sound will be that of leather on wood.

I'm known (generously, in my view) as an 'attacking player' which is a polite way of saying that I couldn't master a forward defensive if I tried. Unlike Larry, the most defensive batsman in the history of the known universe. If you need someone to slash a quick 50, look elsewhere. But if you want someone to anchor one end, Larry is the man -- he will block and prod all day, hour upon hour of grim self-denial as the opposition bowlers lose the will to live. Along with the spectators. As the sun sets and a lone bugler sounds the last post, if you listen closely you can hear the sound of leather on willow. Larry is still at the crease.

But cricket is a game of euphemism. Phrases like "the quick singles seem to have dried up" usually signify that the new batsmen is more than a tad overweight. And although we do not approve of sledging (no sirree), it's important to encourage our bowlers, who make up in imagination what they lack in raw pace -- with an average age of 50, our strike bowlers are not exactly Ambrose and Walsh in their heyday. Often the skipper will toss the ball to Ian or Paul and call for an over or two of 'searing medium pace'. "Good variety Jules" means that the bowler has landed just as many deliveries on the adjacent strip as on the one being used for the match. Even when the bowler has had a shocker, with his previous over lasting 10 balls, a cocktail of wides, no balls, beamers and boundaries we still encourage -- "never mind, we're right behind you Gordon" I call from gully. "Safest bloody place" mutters our wicket keeper under his breath. In the 4th XI 'deceptive pace' translates as 'much slower than you thought'.And I'm not saying that our opposition are pie chuckers, but there is a definite whiff of steak and kidney out on the square somedays.

Despite this, I find myself at the nets at least once a week. Nothing is left to chance in my pursuit of sporting excellence. Last season I even had a brief spell as wicket-keeper. Despite only wearing the gloves for 20 overs, I managed to set a new club record for byes.

As Bones would say - It's cricket Jim, but not as we know it.

29th July 2020 ~ Carry on campers

Camping and I just do not get on. Whenever I am in the vicinity of tents, bad things happen. If there is a camping equivalent of killing an albatross, I must have done it because I am cursed.

Until last weekend I had only previously camped twice in my life. That's not twice in the sense of two holidays but twice in the sense of two nights under canvas. The first was in July 1971 shortly after I had gone to boarding school. As part of what they called Field Day, all junior pupils at the school were expected to take their bicycles and a tent and go as far afield as their little legs would pedal between the end of lessons on Wednesday and prep bell Thursday evening. My intention, being interested in aeroplanes like every 13 year old boy, was to head to RAF Fairford, an airforce base of normally only modest interest. But in 1971, Fairford was the home of Concorde 002, reason enough for 60 mile round trip I felt. So, as the sun set on Wednesday evening, I pitched camp approximately 10 miles from Marlborough in the corner of a wheat field.

My tent was standard army surplus khaki and matched my socks, shoes and trousers, having tripped into a mud puddle up to my knees. On one corner of the tent was a crossed-out shipping label that read "Capetown". Indeed, issued with cadet force army surplus food too, khaki was the colour of the day. Processed cheese, corned beef and sponge pudding - all the colour of khaki. What we were not issued with was any means of cooking the food. Or, in my case, any means of opening the tins. What I would have given for a Swiss Army knife. Rather than stare wistfully at my impregnable K rations, there was nothing to do but turn in for the night.

It was chilly certainly but what I was unprepared for, was the fact that this would be the coldest July night on record. Really. I woke at 3 AM, disorientated with frozen toes and frank hypothermia. There were ice crystals all over the top of the tent and my water flask had frozen. Too cold to sleep, and without any food or water I started cycling. By the time I was in Fairford, Concorde was not, having left for testing in Toulouse. No food, no drink, no Concorde. And if it had been a degree or two colder, probably no toes either.

It was another seven years before I would venture into a tent again, this time in an entirely different circumstance. The Reading Festival with my friend Neil, a gap-toothed biker - and top of the bill that night was Motorhead.

One thing you need to know about rock festivals is that everyone tries to make their tent stand out. So you get everything from tie-dyed army bivouacs and wigwams to Mongolian yurts. Every colour of the rainbow, adorned with flags, ribbons and pennants. Bunting of every kind.. A brilliant plan in many respects except for one tiny little flaw. When you erect your tent it is broad daylight. When you next return to your tent, ears bleeding after the aural handbagging from Motorhead, it is pitch black. And bringing a torch with you is not really very rock 'n' roll. So you have the unenviable task of trying to find your tent amongst row upon row of dark grey shapes or spend hours tripping over guy ropes. Over an hour after Motorhead finished, I finally found my tent and clambered in as quietly as I could in order not wake up Neil or worse still Derek, a part-time Hell's Angel from Ormskirk that Neil had met two years previously at Reading. Not the man that you really wanted to wake unexpectedly from gentle slumber.

In dawn's light it became obvious that the occupants of the tent were not Derek and Neil. It turned out to be Solveig and Ingrid. From Oslo. Only the smell from the overflowing latrines persuaded me that I had not woken in heaven. Still, without a word of Norwegian, I had to explain my presence in their tent. After bewildering the girls with a mix of pidgin, impromptu sign language and semaphore, I shrugged my shoulders and the girls giggled. "Do you speak English?" asked Ingrid in English. Perfect English.

It wasn't me in the wrong tent and the girls were even more apologetic. And articulate. Without resorting to arm flailing, they explained that they been unable to find their tent and had simply picked the first empty one they found. There were just grateful that I had not thrown them out. Inordinately grateful. Just as we were exchanging phone numbers, the tent flap flew open. Neil and Derek had spent their night in the company of two abusive drunks from Auchtermuchty, who had taken a quantity of drugs more commonly associated with bringing down large farm animals. They certainly weren't in the mood to listen to my story and sent me packing back to Reading station. I lost touch with Neil after that. Last I heard, he and Solveig were living on a farm on Orkney. Their eldest son was called Jonathan.

So, last Friday, when Freia and Anton asked us if we would like to share their camping weekend with them, I had to confess that I haven't been camping for 32 years since the Reading Festival debacle. Still, third time lucky? In fairness they sold the idea very attractively. We would be near a vineyard, there was a fine gastropub at the end of the road and the campsite had enough space in the middle of the field to play cricket or football. Sensing a momentary reluctance, they sweetened the deal still further. They would go down to the campsite at lunchtime and set up the tent, while we waltzed in later, in time for Pimms. A good plan by any standard.

Camping has clearly changed in the last 40 years. Gone are the days of khaki Boer War ridge tents, replaced by altogether more exotic species. Our little encampment looked less like the Army of the Potomac, than a mediaeval joust. Tom's tent (he had his own, eschewing an evening under canvas with his sisters) looked like a stealth fighter, while Anton and Freia's tent was about the size of Bodiam Castle. All it lacked were the turrets.

Still, with a glass of Chapel Down champagne in our hands watching the sunset, not much seemed wrong with the world. The rabbit pie followed by syrup pudding was a world removed from the tinned K-rations of 40 years earlier. This was camping that made sense. Not quite Glamping as I understand it but pretty darn good none the less. And listening to the badgers, hedgehogs and foxes through the tent walls almost made my Parkie insomnia worthwhile. The following morning, Freia woke us with hot coffee and bacon sandwiches on homemade zopf, a Swiss milk bread. My faith in camping was restored. Good food, good wine and good company. We were reluctant to leave. But it was Sunday afternoon and we had to get back. There was just time for a country walk and a game of football to help work off those bacon sandwich calories and round off a perfect weekend.

Three hours later, we were home. Well, some of us. Claire was in the garden reassuring the dog, still traumatized by its brief encounter with an electric fence. And I was still waiting in casualty while Alex's broken arm was put in a plaster cast.

Other than that, top weekend!

August

Memory Lane

6th August 2010 ~ Angel

Two decades ago, I worked in Indiana, part of America's almost mythical Midwest. Bloomington, a college town and home of the Hoosiers was little more than a small dab of green paint on a huge agricultural canvas. It was high summer and rain hadn't fallen in nearly six months. Fields, normally, shoulder-high and plump with corn, were dry, bleached flats that stretched out to infinity. When the tractors weren't shimmering in the heat on the open plains, they raised dusty swirls, twists and eddies that glided silently like spectral figures over the distant horizon. Television talked of The Dust Bowl, and those who lived through the 1930s spoke of the similarities and drew anxious parallels. This was the land of Steinbeck, of Tom Joad and the Grapes of Wrath.

Along with friends, I was invited to speak at a conference in Kansas, 500 miles away. We could have flown but chose to drive, in a rattling hired sedan without air conditioning, hour after soporific hour, on arrow-straight undulating roads strung with telegraph poles, the monotony broken only by occasional animal carcasses or rusted flatbeds, abandoned where they had fallen.

"Welcome to nowhere" read the faded graffiti on one decaying Chevy. Through Vincennes, St Louis, Columbia and Independence, and on towards Lawrence on Interstate 70, we played away the hours with tapes of Tom Waits, as we gradually assumed the manners and personae of Kerouac, Cassady and Ginsberg. We left the Interstate, with its honking horns, and set off on a two-lane blacktop. Apart from the trucks, we had the road to ourselves

Night fell swiftly in August on the summer plains and, as the stars filled that ink-black prairie sky, the fuel gauge gradually slipped into the red, and we thumbed the map for our location. Nowhere – just as the graffiti had said. As Joe tapped the fuel gauge, we reached another brow in the road. A flickering sign in the distance read "Food. Gas" with that laconic precision so prevalent throughout the plains states. As the car coughed, we pulled in to a tiny one-pump gas station. It felt like a step back in time. On the far side of the road was a bleached steer skull on a pole. While Joe fuelled the car, Lesley and I stretched our legs, the air still hot from the day. A man in faded overalls and a grease-stained baseball cap emerged from a tiny shack-shop of breeze blocks with a tin roof, kicking the dust as he walked. "Do you have food?" I asked. There was the long pause of a man used to spending his words carefully. "Got all you need there" he said, nodding to the shop "Annie Mae'll help you"

A moth fluttered behind a dirty cracked window next to an antique Coke machine that groaned and burped as its refrigerator fought hopelessly against the heat. A small bell tinkled as I opened the door. Somewhere in the distance the long prairie wail of a goods train pierced the night's silence. I picked Monterey Jack cheese, ham, sesame rolls and rootbeer and placed them on the cracked red Formica counter next to a small tarnished brass bell. As I reached for the bell, there was a rustle of the fly curtain at the back of the shop. "Hello" I called. "Be with you" said a girl's voice. "Annie Mae?" I asked and she smiled, all freckles and dimples, as she totted up the groceries on the corner of a newspaper in her childish hand. She licked the pencil tip then pronounced "That be five dollars and forty three cents". She held up her open hand to signal 'five' and giggled. I saw she was missing a thumb. "Funny girl" I said. She laughed.

I realised my wallet was missing the moment I reached into my trousers and slapped my pockets in the reflex movements of a man unexpectedly penniless. "Vincennes" I said to myself, as I remembered leaving it on the counter of the Dairy Queen, where we had stopped for cones in the late afternoon. Five hours earlier and two hundred miles back on the Interstate. "I have money in the car" I said in explanation. "Back in a minute".

"Well we need to find a bank in the morning" said Lesley "cos I've just spent our last fifteen bucks on gas". Like royalty, Joe never carried money, always relying on Lesley. I explained about the ice cream parlour in Vincennes.

"Annie Mae, I have no money. I'm really sorry" I stuttered and began to put the groceries back. Even in the half light of the shop, my beetroot red face must have been obvious. "It's okay" she said "take the food. You can pay on your way back".

I protested. But Annie Mae would have none of it. "Just don't tell my pop" she winked. And giggled.

As we spluttered out onto the highway again and gathered speed, I told Joe and Lesley about Annie Mae and the food. "Real cute" said Lesley. "Real dumb" said Joe, sparking a row between the two.

We were in Lawrence for two days. Two days hot enough to fry eggs on the bonnet of the car. I did the lecture, with voice barely audible over the air conditioning, my slides buckling in the heat from the projector. I told the listeners of dopamine receptors and the nigrostriatal pathway, of dysregulation and dopamine transporters. Everything I knew about Parkinson's (I used to be a neuroscientist, remember). There were questions too, mostly interested in why an Englishman was in Kansas. "Just following the Yellow Brick Road" I said until it wasn't funny any more. I was shown around the labs, invited to dinner with the faculty members, and guest of honour at a lake party on a bright yellow pontoon boat where we ate slices of watermelon washed down with Coors from the cooler.

Thursday came, muffins and ham for breakfast and then on the road to Nowhere. Or wherever it was that we had stopped for gas and food on Monday night. On a two to one majority, we persuaded Joe to drive back to the garage and give Annie Mae her five dollars and forty three cents, all in shiny new coins. As Joe grumbled and muttered, we looked out for the garage. Mile after mile of dusty emptiness.

Then I saw the cattle skull. We pulled over and I picked up the envelope with the money. The garage looked different. They must have replaced the aged single pump. Two fancy new Texaco pumps stood there.

I looked around. Where was the shop? The breezeblock hut was nowhere. Instead a small glass fronted shop with plastic fittings occupied the space. A middle-aged man emerged. "Need gas?" he asked. "No" I said "I need to give some money to the girl".

He screwed up his eyes. "What girl? Ain't no girl here".

"Annie Mae" I said "Freckles? Missing a thumb".

He looked down and flicked some cigarette ash off his overalls. "She's not here" he said quietly. A long pause. "She'll come around sometimes. When there are strangers mostly".

I waited a moment, but no further explanation was forthcoming. "So where is she now?" I asked.

He nodded in the direction of the corn field opposite. "She bin in the field some twenty years now". His voice faltered. "Buried her there the night her pop brought her in, knocked down by a truck. Folks left their food behind so she ran across the road after them. She was kind like that. Always looking to help. Buried her pop a week later. Wouldn't eat or drink. His little angel she was. Called her Angel Annie somedays".

My mouth was dry and, although he kept talking, I heard nothing else he said as I crossed the road into the field, the corn rustling in the dusty breeze. I reached into my envelope for the five dollars and forty three cents. Shiny new coins glinting in the sun. With a bellow that echoed off the distant grain elevators, I hurled them as far as I could and stood for a moment listening to their pitter patter as they fell among the corn. I turned back towards the car.

From somewhere I heard a giggle.

13th August 2010 ~ Wagner

It is always unsettling to discover you have things in common with notorious characters from history. You might share a birthday with Pol Pot. Or perhaps you have exactly the same Hawaiian shirt as Ferdinand Marcos. Or maybe, like Idi Amin, you have a weakness for Jelly babies. Trivial but embarrassing coincidences. But when you discover, as I did last week, that you share three (yes three) characteristics with Adolf Hitler, the alarm bells do begin to ring somewhat.

The Führer and I certainly share, or shared, an unflappable desire to make the trains run on time. Admittedly my efforts in that direction have amounted to little more than stroppy letters to the management of South Eastern Railways. But goodness knows what might have happened if I'd had the full resources of the Wehrmacht at my disposal. More interestingly, both Hitler and I had Parkinson's. Bearing in mind Hitler's brooding presence in 20th-century world history, you might imagine this fact to be better known. It surprised me. Whilst neither of these two common features are in themselves cause for concern, the third is an altogether guiltier secret. Both Hitler and I share an overwhelming passion for the music of Wagner. And we all know where that can lead.

Before I got married, I even felt the need to confess this love affair to my wife and discovered that sentences starting "Darling, I have a confession ..." aren't always well received, a week before the wedding. But in fairness to Claire, she has learned to share me with Wagner. Admittedly she does periodically check me over for signs of wanting to invade Poland, annex the Sudetenland or any unexpected interest in Volkswagens. And she does get quite twitchy about any stubble left below the nostrils. But as far as I can tell, I've never felt the need to have a Prince Harry moment at any fancy dress party. In any case, I couldn't goosestep if I wanted to.

No composer has been more maligned, no music more misunderstood, no ideology more misrepresented than that of Richard Wagner. Unbelievable perhaps in the light of his championship by Hitler, but Wagner was actually a left-wing Democrat, often on the run for his political views. How could Hitler have failed to notice the key message of all Wagner's music -- the triumph of love over power -- was the antithesis of National Socialism. I mean, how dim can you be.

For someone as passionate about Wagner as myself, this weekend is as close to heaven on earth as I can imagine. All my birthdays and Christmases rolled into one. Because as the weather turns autumnal in the UK, Claire and I are in Bayreuth, a small town in Bavaria and the home of the annual Wagner festival. Nearly 2 months dedicated to the operas of Wagner. Music by Wagner, words by Wagner performed in the opera house built by Wagner. The festival is even run by his great-grandchildren. And if you think tickets for Glyndebourne are hard to obtain, that is nothing compared to the exclusivity of Bayreuth. And we're here to see 'Parsifal' and 'Meistersinger' on consecutive nights. The most sought-after tickets in the world -- there is a 12 year waiting list -- have brought me here for the third, and realistically probably the last, time in my life. I'm not being morbid but merely acknowledging the likelihood that in a decade's time I may well be too disabled, too dyskinetic, or too rigid to sit through operas lasting five hours each without making it a trial for those in adjacent seats.

It's difficult enough without Parkinson's. These are not your run-of-the-mill operas. You know the kind of thing -- a few squeaky arias, a bit of chitchat over a harpsichord and a plot closer to pantomime than drama. You put on your tux, order your interval gin and tonic, and sit down in comfy seats for a couple of hours of mild musical diversion.

Nothing could be further removed from the experience of listening to Wagner at Bayreuth. The sheer size, duration, and intensity of his music makes each opera a feat of endurance. They even last as long as a marathon. And these operas are dangerous. One of his operas, Tristan and Isolde, regularly takes lives: Felix Mottl and Joseph Keilberth both having heart attacks whilst conducting Act 3, at exactly the same point. And if the music does that to its conductor, imagine what it could do to the audience. They should carry a health warning.

And Wagner makes extreme demands of his audience in any opera house, but especially so in my Bayreuth. I know of no other opera house where the audience are locked in for each act (I'm not making this up). Not the place for the claustrophobic. And if you need the toilet -- tough. Think twice before necking that extra Weissbier before Gotterdammerung (The Twilight of the Gods). With a first act over two hours long, and no means of escape, unless you can overpower the German doorman, it could well be the twilight of your underwear. You can almost see them laugh "For you Tommy , ze opera is over". Patrons who faint in the August heat -- there is no air conditioning -- have to recover their composure in their seat, not the bathroom. It is whispered, and I'm in no hurry to test the veracity of the rumour, that patrons who die during the operas -- and there have been a few -- are left in their seats until the end of the act when the stewards presumably go through the auditorium with body bags. Bearing in mind that most of the patrons have waited a lifetime for the tickets, and are therefore perhaps not in the first flush of youth, a certain rate of attrition is perhaps only to be expected. There are always ambulances parked outside the Festspielhaus.

There is no escaping the fact that I'm not in peak physical condition and that this kind of endurance test will be more of a trial with Parkinson's than without. My lifelong propensity to doze off in darkened rooms has been exaggerated by the Parkinson's and the dopamine agonists I take daily. And sitting still makes the blood pool in my legs. The last three operas I've attended have all taken me to Syncope City so the auguries are not good.

But I have a plan -- instead of skipping meals, and fuelling myself on gin and tonics, as I did 20 years ago, I am in training. Plenty of water to stay hydrated in the heat, maybe the odd double espresso to stay awake and glucose tablets to keep my blood sugar up. I shall also be doing exercises throughout the operas, to keep the blood pumping to my brain. Nothing like Mr Motivator, more a regular twiddling of toes and clenching of buttocks. Still probably enough that you wouldn't want the seat next to me. But my trump card cost me £13.99. Flight stockings, and worth every penny.

I've always said I would see Parsifal at Bayreuth and die happy. Just not immediately you understand.

26th August 2010 ~ Sandwich

People have been eating slices of meat in bread since Neolithic times but it was not until John Montagu, the fourth Earl of Sandwich, felt peckish whilst playing cards that this foodstuff acquired its name. Rather than eat meat with his bare hands (as the story goes) Montagu felt the addition of bread would keep the cards free of grease. Evidently the fork, commonplace throughout Western Europe since the 10th century, was a solution beyond the wit of 18th century aristocracy. Eating meat with bare hands indeed – what would his mum say!

I've always thought that our American cousins understand the sandwich better than most. I learnt this in Bloomington Indiana in the mid-80s. At lunchtime, the entire office would parade down to Dagwood's, a tiny basement shop down a rickety iron staircase, where they produced sandwiches unlike any I had ever seen growing up in Doncaster. Each was made to order so it took a few minutes. In any case, the queue stretched up the stairs. And they were worth the wait. Slices of mozzarella, provolone, salami and roast beef formed a platform upon which to pile lettuce, tomatoes, pickled gherkins, olives, chillies, peppers, and ranch dressing. If you ordered 'to go', the entire structure was tightly wrapped in foil, producing a final product that was shaped like a rugby ball and with more chrome than a 1958 Cadillac. Watching Carl, a steroid-fuelled linebacker moonlighting with us over the summer, address a Dagwood's sub was like seeing an anaconda swallow a sheep. I swear he could dislocate his lower jaw. Lord Sandwich would have been dead impressed.

Other than the fact that the Dagwood's sub was called a sandwich, you would struggle to recognise any familial similarity with Lord Montagu's grease sponge or the sarnies that my mother gave me for my school lunch. I always feel sorry for Americans visiting London. In the same way that I was overwhelmed by the US version of the sandwich, Americans must be bewildered by what passes for a sandwich on this side of the pond. A slice of processed ham, the thickness of a microscopy specimen, between two slices of steam baked white loaf must seem at best a poor joke if not a downright insult. But then in Britain, a sandwich is an apology -- a way of saying "I'm not really hungry but I suppose I'd better eat something". And if you eat anything with that attitude, you deserve to face disappointment. In America, the sandwich says "Boy am I hungry!"

But if we accept for a second that the sandwich is a British invention, it all makes sense. Because I can't help thinking that the sandwich is rather like football. Basically we, that is the British, invent the thing and, while sitting on our laurels, fail to notice that everyone else in the world is getting better at it. Then before we know it, everyone else's sandwiches are better than our own. We are no longer in the premiership. Over the centuries we have gradually slipped out of the sandwich elite. Thank goodness there is no Sandwich World Cup.

I'm glad to say that my time in the States imbued me with a genuine grasp of what a sandwich could be, a sense of sandwich adventure if you will. My friend Werner had a very simple definition. If the sandwich would fit through a letterbox, it wasn't a sandwich worthy of the name. Certainly there was no way a Dagwoods Hoosier Deli Sub would go through a letterbox. It was difficult enough getting it through a door.

The wife says I eat too much bread generally and harps on about types of carbohydrate. Apparently there are good and bad sorts of carbs. Something to do with glycaemic index or similar (actually I should get her to write this part, she is a diabetes nurse). And my sandwiches are invariably always made with the wrong sort of bread. So before I have even opened the fridge door, my sandwich has not even made it past the blueprint stage without comment. And let's not forget, this is just a sandwich not a new supersonic airliner. Two slices of bread -- how can that be bad?

I've always been fond of sandwiches -- in my view, they represent a blank canvas. A chance for the sandwich artist to express himself with imaginative ingredients as an artist would use pigments. When I was a kid, there was no ingredient combination that I would not try. Whatever was in the fridge was fair game. Double and even triple decker sandwiches overflowing with creativity and ketchup. Ok it was not exactly the Sistine Chapel roof but then if Michelangelo had run your local Subway, who knows. I even gave the sandwiches names, recalling our holiday in New York in 1966. The "Salami Surprise", "Cheese Squeeze" and "Ham Slam" were self-explanatory.

But all this talk of sandwiches makes me hungry. Time to renew my acquaintance with "The Beast" ...

September

Saying Goodbye

15th September 2010 ~ Leaving home

A rite of passage certainly. The biggest change in our family life yet. But there was no ceremony, no fanfares, nothing to mark the event. A hug, a peck on the cheek and into the car. Catherine, my baby, was off to college. Seconds later, the car had vanished round the corner and I found myself still waving at nothing. A neighbour emerged. "Are you okay?" he asked. "Yes thanks" I said, managing something like a smile, and turned indoors to regain my composure.

I remember with crystal clarity that night Catherine was born, 18 years ago yet as fresh a memory as yesterday. Where did those 18 years go? Did I blink?

Catherine had been packing for weeks -- everything she would need for college. Pots and pans, pillows and duvet, music, laptop, iPod, and chocolate. Weeks dominated by boxes, bags and lists. Lists of every shape and form -- things to take, things to make and things to bake. Shopping, shaping and shipping. Labels, tables and cables. In fact as far as I can tell, she has taken more or less the entire contents of her bedroom, presumably intending to recreate it in detail at college. She hasn't really left home at all -- because the home appears to have left with her. All that remains in her room are half eaten chocolate bars and empty bags of crisps. Oh and an unmade bed, leaving the dislocating illusion that she has just gone to the bathroom.

When I went to boarding school 30 years ago, my mother wept incessantly. From Wiltshire to Doncaster was a good four hours by road and, after leaving me at the school gates, my mother cried every minute of the journey home. My father, one hand on the wheel and eyes fixed in steely gaze on the road ahead, would say nothing but wring out handkerchief after handkerchief, lost in his own thoughts. Even when she had apparently finished, the family was still not out of the woods. Any sad story on television or in the newspaper would be enough to set her off again. For days after the beginning of term, my mother never left the house without a handkerchief. And the sight of my mother sobbing could signify anything from a news item about abandoned kittens to a dip in the stock market. There was simply no way of knowing. The family were treading on eggshells.

But four decades ago there was no e-mail, no instant communication to soften the palpable weight of separation. Written communication meant envelopes and stamps, words on paper. And handwritten words at that. Typewriters were clunky mechanical leviathans of keys, ink and ribbon and the idea of domestic word processors was still a good decade away. So pen and paper it had to be. Or the telephone. The public telephone that is -- a grimy, chewing gum encrusted booth, sour with urine and peeling stickers advertising services that, at 13, I could barely imagine. Phone calls were punctuated by beeps and tinkles as more coins were inserted. With hindsight it would have irritated Alexander Graham Bell. The mobile phone was barely a twinkle in some geek's eye. And as for Skype, it's probably just as well it wasn't around 40 years ago to see my mother blubbing on the other end of the phone.

By the time I went to college, six years later, my mother had done all the crying she needed.

So on Friday, we set the table for four people not five. Four plates, four glasses, four knives and four forks. I moved from my normal place at the head of the table to Catherine's. We didn't say anything. We didn't need to. Supper was a little quieter than normal, Alice and Alex not yet adjusted to the changes, neither ready yet to step up to the plate. Big changes, big adjustments to be made.

But at least I can get in the bathroom now.

21st September 2010 ~ Vegetroubles

I learnt from an early age to harbour a deep mistrust of all recipes that involved the word 'surprise'. As in 'courgette surprise', 'celery surprise' or, worst of all, 'broad bean surprise' which embodied all my worst food nightmares in a single dish comprised, as best I could tell with fingers clenched over my nostrils, solely of broad beans. And nothing else. To this day, like the search for the enigma in Elgar's famous set of variations, I don't know what the surprise was. In any case, speculation is fruitless as my mother thankfully took the recipe -- if indeed there was one -- to the grave.

In fairness, the 'surprise' recipes were only one more weapon in a constant battle by my mother to get her children to eat more vegetables. We had long since passed the stage where carrots and green beans were "orange chips" and "green chips". Even to the untutored palette of a three-year-old, that was never going to wash. But in the long litany of culinary mendacity, these were small felonies, misdemeanours on a par with "it tastes like chicken".

On the whole, things didn't taste like chicken. Not rabbit, guinea fowl, turkey gizzards, song thrushes, frogs legs or any of the many untranslatable items my parents seemed to find on foreign menus. As my parents found to their cost on many a foreign holiday, we were not going to be duped. The same scene was repeated in every restaurant from Cannes to Calais, from Marseille to Montmartre in an effort to persuade us children to eat, or at least contemplate eating, unfamiliar nameless dishes. While my mother made distracting small talk, my father would thumb through Baedeker before confidently pronouncing that a terrine of sand eels would be indistinguishable from chicken breast on the palate. In desperate situations, he would resort to collusion with the waiter. "Veree good choice monsieur, eet taste like chicken" he would say as I unwittingly ordered a plate of mixed goat offal.

Under most circumstances, the vegetarian option would be considered a safe choice when faced with menu items that would strike fear in the strongest of hearts. After all, how antagonistic can an onion quiche be? Alas this option was not available to my parents. Like most children, I detested vegetables. I just didn't see the point of them.

"Jonathan can be a bit fussy" my mother would say to the parents of any child foolish enough to invite me back to their house for tea. Sometimes, in an effort to stave off trouble, she would wearily present them with handwritten lists of proscribed foods.

I blame school dinners. Cauldrons of vegetables cooked to the point where all nutritional value was gone. Along with any colour. Or flavour. Or indeed identifying marks. After three hours of boiling, most vegetables took on a sort of battleship grey hue. This was strangely fitting in a dining hall decorated with faded pictures of the Battle of Jutland. The long refectory tables were even reputed to have come from HMS Warspite. But since they seemed to be constructed of railway sleepers, the Doncaster locomotive works was probably the more likely source.

Until you have tasted cabbage cooked for three hours, you have no concept of the depths to which institutional catering could sink. It was almost transubstantiation in reverse. With the power of faith, a glass of wine could become the blood of Christ. With the power of an industrial boiler the size of a bath, fresh green cabbages could become the kind of grey slurry that would have caused even Oliver Twist to think twice.

So for most of the last 50 odd years, I have treated vegetables as a necessary evil, generally eschewing seconds. At best I have a grudging acceptance of their necessity. Even more so nowadays, as Parkinson's seems to predispose its victims to constipation. "Vegetables will help you live longer" says my wife cheerily, piling more broccoli onto my plate. "No, it just seems longer" I mutter.

I have a natural antipathy to the many manifestations of the lentil tendency. I lose track of the number of restaurants which serve dishes accompanied by a "medley of seasonal vegetables", "a symphony of sprouts and sorrel" or some such pretentious tosh. My hackles rise at anything which purports to give vegetables airs and graces.

So with my natural resistance to the presence of green foodstuffs on my plate, you will perhaps be surprised to learn that I am a convert. Like Saul on the road to Damascus, I have seen the vegetable light. And bizarrely, this conversion occurred in a Mongolian yurt, near Maidstone.

I'm not making this up.

A couple of weeks ago, Freia and Anton suggested that we went out together for dinner. So far so good. But not just anywhere. Apparently, despite no shortage of local restaurants, we were to head to a farmer's field near Maidstone where some enterprising chappies had put up a tent and planned to feed us from a field kitchen. Visions of post-war national service sprang to mind. And were it not for the very detailed instructions, I would have taken it for a prank.

When the satnav abandoned us among fruit trees and muddy fields, I was convinced we had been set up. But as our eyes adjusted to the darkness, it became clear that there was indeed a large tent among the trees. Freia gave me one of her "there, I told you so" looks and I was grudgingly forced to concede that, so far, this matched exactly her description of what was in store. Inside the tent -- which was indeed, as billed, a Mongolian yurt -- was a throng of earnest, veggie types. Your basic nightmare. As designated driver, I couldn't even adopt my usual solution to this sort of situation -- to drink myself into a coma.

But what followed was a revelation. There was no menu -- they simply placed eight dishes on the table and we shared amongst ourselves and our neighbours. All of the food was organic, all was fresh and local and all was delicious. And there's next to no use in describing the names of the dishes, because they were cooked with such passion that they were elevated way above their names. After a stupefying plum crumble, chocolate brownies and a sort of Eton mess, I could hardly breathe, let alone move.

We were almost the last to leave, as they were packing up the yurt. Freia and Claire were deluged with flowers and more vegetables. Most bizarrely of all, I found myself discussing the recipes on the way home.

I have seen the promised land. And it's organic.

27th September 2010 ~ Taking stock

When people ask I say I have had Parkinson's for nearly 4 years. Well that's untrue of course -- what I mean is that I was diagnosed with Parkinson's 4 years ago. Not quite the same thing since, like most of us, there was a period when I had symptoms that had yet to be pieced together into a firm diagnosis. But for convenience sake, let's say I've had it for 4 years. So it's probably time to take stock and look at the ways in which it has changed my life. And the ways in which it hasn't.

Everyone's Parkinson's is different. Tremor, rigidity, akinesia and postural instability are the four basic ingredients. But like a cocktail, their proportions vary. And even with the same balance of ingredients, the same combination of symptoms, the results will differ according to the individual. A dry martini at Harry's bar in Venice will not be the same drink as a dry martini at the Opera house bar in Sydney.

There is a natural tendency among people with Parkinson's, and I imagine it generalises to other chronic illnesses, to make comparisons. To look at each other's symptoms and compare our relative progress. It's only natural. But such comparisons are largely futile. You and I are different. My Parkinson's has doubtless progressed differently from yours in the last four years. And four years from now, we will be different again.

Some forms of Parkinson's are particularly brutal, swiftly incapacitating their sufferers. Others are mild, with little change year on year. Some of us respond well to our treatments, others suffer side-effect after side-effect. There's simply no way of telling, of predicting this. The progression of Parkinson's seems to be stepwise too, for me at least. Months go by without change and then suddenly, over the space of a week or two, I will be aware that my shakes are much worse or that I am shuffling more. Some days you would not know I had Parkinson's. On others, you would wonder how I managed to dress myself.

Shortly after I was diagnosed, I saw a letter from my consultant to another discussing my case. My hospital has a policy of copying healthcare letters to me, a policy which may or may not extend to other health authorities. I had been referred for a DATscan on the grounds that I had a "rather progressive" form of Parkinson's. If they were describing anything other than Parkinson's, I would take that to be positive."Progressive" suggests forwardthinking. I think of progressive rock -- of Emerson Lake and Palmer. Positive images on the whole. But of course the word had a different meaning here. "Progressive" was shorthand for "rapidly deteriorating". That was four years ago.

So have I? Deteriorated rapidly that is? Am I where my consultants expected me to be? That's hard to answer. Since that first meeting with my consultant, when he discussed my case earnestly and enthusiastically with me, I have not seen him since. My second hospital visit was handled by a senior registrar. Since then, I have only been seen by a parade of registrars. And so many that their names elude me. We meet each six months for 10 minutes, they take a hurried snapshot of my life, and we go our separate ways. They learn as little about me as I do about them.

So let me do this myself. My UPDRS (self-assessed) is 34 and my Hoehn and Yahr score is 2.5.

But let's turn those numbers into something that reflects me, what I can do and what I cannot.

Probably the most affected aspect is my handwriting. In the space of four years this has gone from clear, steady and legible to the point where even writing cheques is a chore. I can rarely write more than a couple of lines at a time, so it is hard to take notes in a lecture for instance. Sometimes I will ask others to write things down for me.

Typing is a little better, but still prone to typos from my flapping hands. It's better in the mornings. Touch screens such as on the iPad are particularly problematic. Since my tremor is worse on the dominant side, I've taken to typing left-handed when the shakes are particularly bad. Not ideal, but not impossible either. I sometimes feel a little like a child learning to type.

When the tremors are bad, mealtimes can be embarrassing. But I've learnt to put the glass of wine down when I start shaking uncontrollably. The same goes for food. When the shakes mean that I risk piercing my lip with a fork, I simply put the fork down and wait. There can be a lot of waiting. If we are in a restaurant and I have ordered injudiciously, my wife Claire will discreetly cut my food into manageable pieces. She can usually tell when I'm struggling.

These are the activities of daily living, the activities our neurologists used to assess our debility. Generally speaking, it paints a picture -- in my case at least -- of probably moderate illness severity. It even speaks of impaired quality of life for instance. But this is where I take issue with the assessment scales. The focus is unduly on what I can't do. And if writing, typing and eating were all I did, that would be fair enough. But they're not. Nor do they capture the essence of me and what matters to me. They are irritations, nothing more. And I will find ways around them. So enough of what I can't do, or can't do well. And let's nip that 'quality of life' talk in the bud while we're at it.

What matters to me? Family, discovering new music, watching the opera, experimental cooking, friends who see me not my shakes, Wagner, tracing my ancestors, watching and playing cricket, driving the Jag, maps, neuroscience, smelly cheeses, family birthdays, French holidays, cookbooks, language and languages, Hammer horror films, listening and talking, power tools, fruit smoothies, Christmas, astronomy evenings with my telescope, vintage claret, local history, strong coffee, making glass bowls and panels, canal boats, Yorkshire, malt whisky, writing this book, holidays, home-made bread, gadgets, reading for pleasure, fundraising for Parkinson's, Scrabble, walks in the countryside, dogs, black and white photography and chocolate.

So -- things I can't do very well - 3, things I can still enjoy - 40.

I'd say my glass was half full. At least half full.

The Last Word

4th October 2010 ~ The promised land

When you want something badly enough, fear of the future evaporates in the face of the needs of the immediate.

On 3 April 1968, at the height of the African-American civil rights protests, the Rev Martin Luther King addressed a nervous crowd at the Mason Temple in Memphis. Racists had threatened his life, and those of his followers. The smell of fear was in the air. But King, like the calm at the eye of the storm, stuck to his guns. He concluded his speech, even by his own standards a breathtaking piece of oratory, with the following beautiful words

"We've got some difficult days ahead. But it really doesn't matter with me now, because I've been to the mountaintop. Like anybody, I would like to live a long life. Longevity has its place. But I'm not concerned about that now. I just want to do God's will. And He's allowed me to go up to the mountain. And I've looked over. And I've seen the Promised Land. I may not get there with you. But I want you to know tonight, that we, as a people, will get to the promised land!"

His words were prophetic, on two counts. The following evening King was assassinated, his death fanning the flames of the civil rights movement to an unquenchable inferno. King had not only shown his people the way, but he had gone on ahead to the promised land.

For King, the promised land was the emancipation of his people. For others, the promised land comes in different shapes and forms. For people with Parkinson's, the promised land would be nothing less than a cure, a release from our symptoms.

I may be no King but I too have have glimpsed the promised Parky land. Let me explain. On Monday, I caught a flight to Glasgow. The plane was late leaving and, even after a hair raising taxi ride from the airport, it was still midnight before I arrived at the hotel. Just time to savour a large Lagavulin before turning in for the night in the not unreasonable hope that the whisky might stave off the persistent insomnia that seems to dog me these days. I was wrong. A little before five, I was staring at the ceiling, my head buzzing with ideas and thoughts. There was no use trying to sleep. I got up, checked Facebook and e-mails and picked up the conference program.

The conference in question was the 2nd World Parkinson Congress. To the casual observer, this was a conference much like any other. Some 3000 delegates from 50 odd countries, all with an interest in movement disorders. And the usual mix of pharmaceutical companies, device manufacturers, booksellers and charities all vying for delegates' attention. But this congress was different because it was attended not only by physicians and scientists, but also by patients. Like me. The whole Parkinson's community. All talked and all listened. We heard about gene polymorphisms, about synucleinopathies, of gene slice variants, and everything else besides. Above all, the buzz was of disease modification and neuroregenerative strategies. That's 'cure' to you and me. Yes there have been many false dawns but the sense of anticipation was palpable. The scientists carry the burden of our expectations. And we told them so.

But, above all, I have met people who will change my life forever. People just starting their Parkinson's journey, open eyed, open-minded and openmouthed at the future. People who still find time to give to others, even when their PD has taken nearly everything. I have seen people who daily face nameless fears with unimaginable courage. I have seen people stand with dignity against the many cruel indignities of this condition.

In the end, nobody understands Parkinson's better than fellow sufferers. Parkinson's is an individual journey, and at the same time a journey of individuals. Better than any medicine is the knowledge that I will make this journey with friends. We will stumble together along the shore. And though we come from different lands, speak different languages, we are one family – brothers and sisters in this struggle.

This week I have seen my greatest hopes and worst fears both made real. I have peered into the darkest shadows and blinked against the brightness of the light. But out of it all, I acknowledge one fact - the future will be about a cure. It has to be about a cure. There will be a day when we will reach those broad sunlit uplands, where we will stride not stumble, stretch not stiffen and finally be at peace with our still bodies. And we will walk there together, holding each other's hands, from darkness to light.

This congress was the mountaintop from which the Parky future is visible. We will reach the promised land.